Bond

CW00959401

How to do ...

11+ Non-verbal Reasoning

Alison Primrose

Nelson Thornes

Text © Alison Primrose 2002, 2007
Original illustrations © Nelson Thornes Ltd 2002, 2007

The right of Alison Primrose to be identified as author of this work has been asserted by her in accordance with the Copyright, Designs and Patents Act 1988.

All rights reserved. No part of this publication may be reproduced or transmitted in any form or by any means, electronic or mechanical, including photocopy, recording or any information storage and retrieval system, without permission in writing from the publisher or under licence from the Copyright Licensing Agency Limited, of Saffron House, 6-10 Kirby Street, London, EC1N 8TS.

Any person who commits any unauthorised act in relation to this publication may be liable to criminal prosecution and civil claims for damages.

First published in 2002 by:
Nelson Thornes Ltd

This edition published in 2007 by:
Nelson Thornes Ltd
Delta Place
27 Bath Road
CHELTENHAM
GL53 7TH
United Kingdom

13 / 10

A catalogue record for this book is available from the British Library

ISBN 978 0 7487 8121 8

Illustrations by Bede Illustration
Page make-up by Wearset Ltd

Printed in China by 1010 Printing International Ltd

Contents

Standard 11+ Non-verbal Reasoning Test
(Central pull-out section)

Introduction

Non-verbal reasoning is a popular tool that can be used in a variety of ways to test aptitude levels in children and adults. As adults, we may come across it as part of an interview process for jobs in fields such as engineering, design or science, as these areas involve working with visual information. For children, it forms a common element of the 11+/selective entrance examinations process for many UK grammar and independent secondary schools.

Although it is not taught as a discrete curriculum subject at primary school, the understanding and skills that underpin non-verbal reasoning are integral to teaching and learning in a range of subjects, particularly maths, science, design and technology. Non-verbal reasoning does not rely on having strong literacy skills, as all questions are in pictorial or diagrammatic form. As a result, it is regarded by many secondary schools as a fairer, more reliable indicator of potential academic ability than English-based tests.

The selective secondary school entry process is likely to be the first point at which children will encounter non-verbal reasoning as a specific test. This book is therefore a vital resource for all children preparing for the 11+ or other secondary school entrance exams.

(1) What is an 11+ non-verbal reasoning exam?

Unlike most other exams, selective entrance tests cannot be retaken. There is no second chance at the 11+ (although some schools do still set exams for entry at 12 or 13+), so there is always fierce competition and pressure around these exams.

The scope and content of an 11+ non-verbal reasoning test can often differ across UK regions, as there is a range of question types that can be included. However, a paper will generally be testing a child's ability to:

- process graphic or pictorial information
- apply logical thinking and problem-solving skills
- understand how objects relate to each other in space (spatial awareness)
- find and follow patterns and rules
- apply maths skills – rotation, reflection, symmetry
- work systematically.

An 11+ non-verbal reasoning paper can be written in two formats, following either a **multiple-choice** or **standard** layout. For a multiple-choice paper, children will need to choose their answer from a set of options and mark it on a separate answer sheet. Answers must be marked in these booklets very carefully as the answer sheets are often read and marked by a computerised system. In the standard format, children must write each answer directly onto the question paper.

As with all exams 11+ non-verbal reasoning papers are timed, typically lasting between 45 minutes and one hour. The introduction of a timeframe can often have a negative impact on a child's performance, so it is important for children to work through practice materials in both timed and non-timed environments.

② How can you use this book?

How to do … 11+ Non-verbal Reasoning is designed for use by children who are preparing for non-verbal reasoning exams, but it also includes many helpful tips and suggestions for adults who are supporting them in the process. It presents a wider selection of question types than are likely to appear on an exam paper and this provides children with a significant strategic advantage. Learning and practising as many different question types as possible greatly reduces the potential for them to be faced with 'surprises' during an exam.

This step-by-step tutorial resource can be worked through, section by section, from start to finish. However, if your child is already proficient with several question types he or she may only need to work through particular types in full. The short test at the start of each main section can help to highlight which question types your child may need additional practice on and the detachable test can also be a useful starting point. The easy-to-use structure of *How to do … 11+ Non-verbal Reasoning* also means that it can be kept as a reference tool to look up the key strategies that will solve those tricky practice questions which may have your child (and you!) stumped.

How to do … 11+ Non-verbal Reasoning is part of the well-known and long-established Bond series, whose finely-graded 11+ resources have been used and trusted by parents, teachers and tutors for over 40 years. This title accompanies the full range of *Bond Assessment Papers* and *11+ Test Papers* in non-verbal reasoning, which provide thorough practice of all key question types explained in this manual. From age 9 to 12+, these practice materials also include a simple cross-referencing system to *How to do … 11+ Non-verbal Reasoning,* so the right strategy can be identified to work out every question. As this book covers a wide range of question types, it can also be used to complement all other non-verbal reasoning practice test papers.

③ How is this book organised?

There is a range of different non-verbal reasoning question types that need to be mastered in order to succeed in 11+, 12+ and 13+ selective entrance exams. However, several types rely on and test the same basic skills so it is often easier to learn similar types together. The question types included in this step-by-step guide are therefore organised in groups according to the skills that underpin them, so that each skills set can be reinforced and similar question types can be easily identified.

There are three main sections to this book:

A Where do you start?
B The key non-verbal reasoning question types
C How do you prepare for the exam?

Section A provides clear guidance on the fundamental knowledge and basic skills every child needs to have before starting more focused non-verbal reasoning practice. The tips in this section give essential advice on how to check and improve your child's basic reasoning skills, as well as raise his or her attainment in some key maths topics. Further guidance for supporting your child's maths skills specifically can be found in *How to do … 11+ Maths*.

Section B covers a wide range of key question types that may appear on a non-verbal reasoning exam:

- **similarities** (2 versions)
- **analogies**
- **sequences**
- **hidden shapes**
- **matrices**
- **reflected shapes**
- **nets of cubes**
- **codes**
- **combined shapes.**

These 10 essential types are organised into groups under four main headings: **Identifying shapes**, **Missing shapes**, **Rotating shapes** and **Coded shapes and logic**.

Each of these four parts begins with a short test that is designed to identify how much your child already understands about the question types introduced in that segment of the book. If your child scores well, he or she may not need to work through the question types in full but should reinforce existing knowledge by reading through all the **Remember** boxes and final **Top Tips!** checklist. If each short test is completed in pencil, it can then be retaken, if necessary, once your child has worked through a section in full. Two score boxes are provided at the bottom of each test so 'before and after' scores can be compared.

For those who need more support, each group of question types provides:

- practical step-by-step explanations and worked examples for each type
- practice questions to check what has been learnt
- essential advice and hints for both children and parents.

Only one method of tackling a question type is given for most examples. There may be other ways of approaching a particular type but the techniques given here are felt to be the most straightforward and practical for children to learn.

Section C provides further guidance for pre-exam preparation and for the day itself.

The **central pull-out section** contains a full-length 11+ non-verbal reasoning practice paper, based on Bond's standard format *11+ Test Papers*. It covers many of the key question types likely to appear on an exam paper, all of which are included in

How to do … 11+ Non-verbal Reasoning. If you wish to set this paper as a 'before and after' test, then please visit www.bond11plus.co.uk and follow the Free Resources link to download another copy. The answers to the test are at the end of the **Answers** section, which also includes the solutions to the four section tests and all practice questions.

To accompany this book, some **free electronic materials** are also available for you to download from our web site at www.bond11plus.co.uk. Where online materials are available, the following icon appears in the margin:

④ When should you start practising?

It is difficult to specify the exact period of time your child will need to practise for these exams as all children are different. Some children will pass a non-verbal reasoning selective entrance exam without having completed many practice papers. Others may have worked towards it for two years and still not achieve the necessary standard. However, as a guide, start to encourage some light skills practice (logic puzzles and visual brainteasers, for example) about 18 months before the test date (during the summer term of Year 4). Starting this early will allow plenty of time for your child to reinforce their general reasoning skills before moving on to learn the key skills and techniques involved in solving each question type.

This is also the ideal time to set the non-verbal reasoning placement tests found in *The Parents' Guide to the 11+*. These unique papers will assess your child's ability level and help you to develop an individual learning plan for your child (whether you have two years or three months to go before the exam). They will also show you which practice materials will be the most appropriate for your child to work through.

Once you have 12 months or less to go, it is important to establish a regular weekly routine for practice – little and often is usually best. This needs to be planned carefully to fit in with school homework. Many children are tired at the end of the school day, so a fixed time slot first thing on a Saturday or Sunday morning can often be a good time. Using the detachable test at the centre of this book at this stage can help you to see how your child copes with a range of common question types. Remember to keep your copy of *How to do … 11+ Non-verbal Reasoning* handy once you start regular practice sessions.

⑤ What do you need?

Checklist

- ✓ A ready supply of **pencils** and **erasers**.
- ✓ A pad of **spare paper** for rough working.
- ✓ A **clock** for timed work.
- ✓ A quiet, **well-lit area** in which to practise.

✓ PARENT TIP

A shopping excursion for items such as a special notebook, some pencils and highlighter pens can be a great motivator to start your child on test practice!

For particular question types you may also find a **small mirror**, **tracing paper** and examples of **3D shapes** (such as dice) useful.

A: Where do you start?

(1) Check general ability

Before you set your child off on specific 11+ exam practice, it is a good idea to assess current ability levels. This will ensure that both you and your child are confident that the 11+ is a realistic aim and will also provide a clear foundation from which to practise more advanced techniques.

No one element of assessment can give a complete picture of your child's ability, but if you combine several factors (see below for suggestions) you will be able to gain a much clearer sense of the level your child has already achieved.

○ Talk to your child's teacher.
Find out what your child's predicted results are for the Year 6 SATs (National Curriculum Tests). At what level is your child working in all subjects? By the end of Year 6, children are expected to reach level 4 in subjects such as English, maths and science. The 11+ exam papers are likely to be set with this as a minimum competency level, and some may be set higher. Make sure you read through all recent school reports and clarify any queries, so you can gain a sense of your child's overall level of achievement.

Ask the teacher to confirm your child's reading age. The higher this is above his or her actual age, the greater advantage your child will have when tackling selective entrance exams.

○ Set some timed practice tests.
If you give your child some preliminary timed tests, you will be able to assess the appropriate level at which he or she will need to start practising. Using the scores from these tests as a starting point, you will also be able to track progress once you begin a programme of more focused practice.

The unique **placement tests** in *The Parents' Guide to the 11+* have been designed specifically for this purpose. They have been created by an experienced 11+ tutor and form the initial part of a tried-and-tested, well-structured assessment process. Using these will highlight any weak areas of knowledge and allow you to develop an individual plan for your child.

You can also use the detachable full-length paper at the centre of this book as a 'before and after' test if you set a timeframe of 30 minutes on each occasion. (A free second copy of the test can be downloaded from our web site. Follow the Free Resources link at www.bond11plus.co.uk)

② *Check basic reasoning skills*

Have you noticed if your child has shown a natural interest and aptitude for logic puzzles, problem solving and spatial awareness? The ability to think logically, analyse images, spot common links, patterns, differences or rules, relate objects to space and work systematically are all essential skills in understanding non-verbal reasoning questions. So how can you support these skills?

○ Reinforce key maths concepts.
Several question types are underpinned by some key maths skills, so it will be beneficial to strengthen your child's understanding in these areas before working through any practice papers. In particular, your child needs to be comfortable working with:

✓ angles
✓ reflection
✓ lines of symmetry
✓ rotation
✓ 3D shapes.

See under 'Play games' below, read the relevant tips in section B and look through *How to do ... 11+ Maths* for advice on how to support understanding and skills in these as well as other key maths topics.

○ Play games.
Playing games and solving puzzles is one of the best ways to improve observation and reasoning skills as well as to develop spatial awareness. Children are often more receptive to learning when they don't realise that's what they're doing!

Foster these skills by encouraging your child to:
✓ complete jigsaws and sliding piece puzzles (complex pictures and numerous pieces will create more of a challenge)
✓ work out spot-the-difference puzzles (the more detail in an image, the greater the test)
✓ decipher visual brainteasers – try one a day over breakfast
✓ play tiling games involving tetrominoes (Tetris®, for example) or pentominoes (such as Katamino). These types of puzzle are widely available for most games consoles and are often found on mobile phones. They promote spatial awareness and can also support your child's understanding of key maths concepts: rotation, symmetry, nets, area, perimeter and volume
✓ unravel other maths-based logic puzzles which can help to develop spatial awareness as well as strengthen basic maths abilities (Sudoku and Kakuro, for example)
✓ assemble 3D interlocking or shape-building puzzles and construct 3D modelling kits
✓ solve dissection puzzles such as tangrams. These Chinese puzzles encourage spatial awareness and problem-solving skills as they consist of seven geometric shapes that, when put together correctly, form a rectangle or a square. They can also be positioned in various outlines to form other shapes (such as an animal or person). Ready-made tangram sets are widely available or you can have fun together making your own out of stiff card
✓ crack a Rubik's Cube®!

Find further ideas for games and puzzles in the parents' tips throughout section B, in the puzzles sections of Bond's *10 Minute Tests in Non-verbal Reasoning* and *Maths* and at www.beam.co.uk

B: The key non-verbal reasoning question types

Identifying shapes

This group of question types tests your understanding and recognition of shape and pattern. It relies on:

- your ability to find shapes that are similar or different
- your skills for sorting given shapes or symbols according to their common features.

Try this test to find out how many identifying shapes question types you can already do. Circle the letter representing your chosen option for each question.

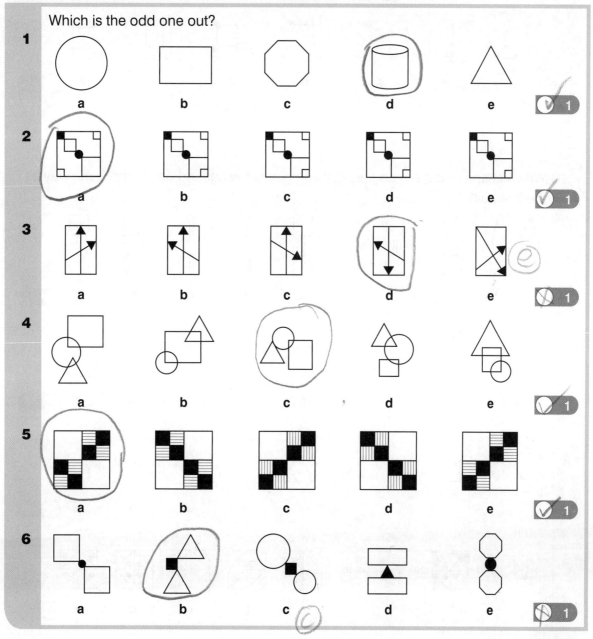

Which is the odd one out?

Which pattern on the right belongs in the group on the left?

7

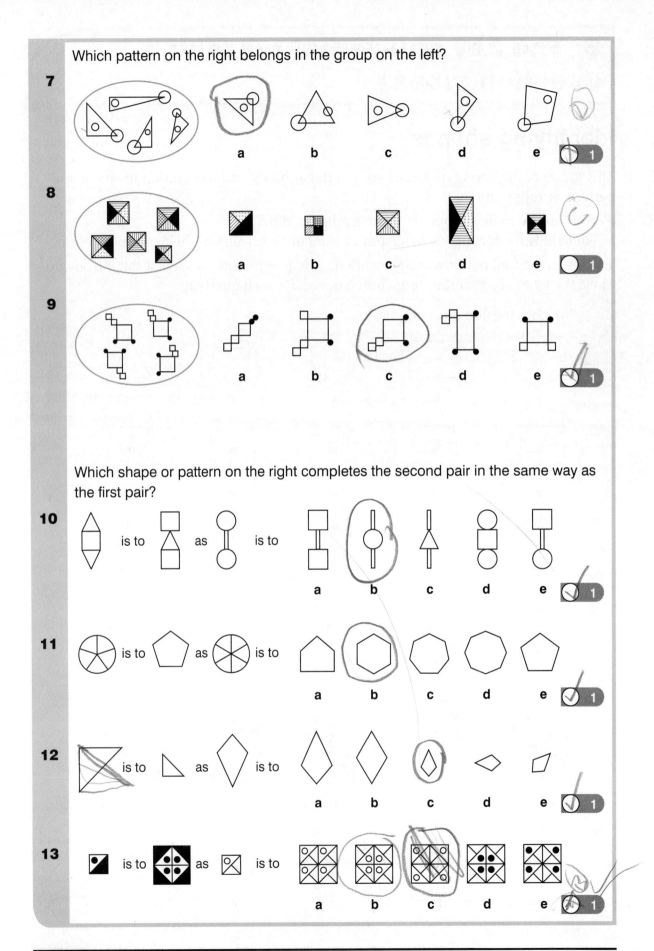

a   b   c   d   e   1

8

a   b   c   d   e   1

9

a   b   c   d   e   1

Which shape or pattern on the right completes the second pair in the same way as the first pair?

10

a   b   c   d   e   1

11

a   b   c   d   e   1

12

a   b   c   d   e   1

13

a   b   c   d   e   1

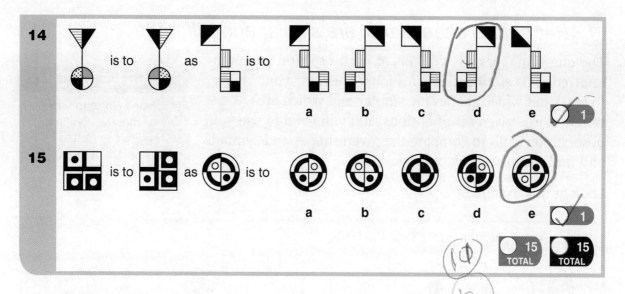

14 ⬇ is to ⬇ as ◰ is to **a** ◰ **b** ◰ **c** ◰ **d** ◰ **e** ⊘ 1

15 ⊞ is to ⊞ as ◉ is to **a** ◉ **b** ◉ **c** ◉ **d** ◉ **e** ⊘ 1

◯ 15 TOTAL ◯ 15 TOTAL

How did you do?

- Thirteen or more correct? Read the **Top Tips!** and then go on to the next section: Missing shapes.
- Twelve or fewer correct? Work through the question types in this section carefully and then retake the test!

What types of features or links could objects or symbols have in common? You may need to consider any or all of the following elements:

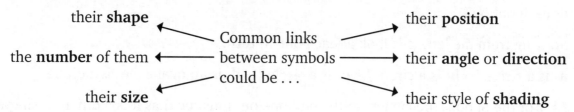

their **shape**

their **position**

the **number** of them ← Common links between symbols could be . . . → their **angle** or **direction**

their **size**

their style of **shading**

A common link between shapes may not be immediately obvious. It may not always be a visible feature, so make sure you write down as many ideas as you can think of!

There are three main sets of identifying shapes question types. These are:

- Recognise shapes that are similar and different.
- Identify shapes and patterns.
- Pair up shapes.

Let's work through this group of question types, looking at each set in turn.

 **PARENT TIP**

Help your child to develop their understanding of visual connections and observation skills. Collect a group of objects and ask your child to identify the odd one out. Then ask him or her to explain the link between the remaining objects. For example: a biro, a felt tip pen, a crayon, a pencil, an eraser. The eraser is the odd one out; the other four are linked by function – they are writing implements. Or: a golf ball, a tennis ball, a rugby ball, a football, a basketball. The rugby ball is the odd one out; the other four.are linked by shape – they are spheres.

① Recognise shapes that are similar and different

The question types we will look at in this section are often referred to as **similarities** questions. They test your ability to work out which shapes are similar and which are different in a given set of options. You will need to use your observation skills to compare the given shapes and symbols and find the visual link or links.

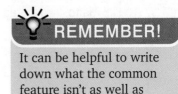
REMEMBER!

It can be helpful to write down what the common feature isn't as well as what it might be!

Look at this example.

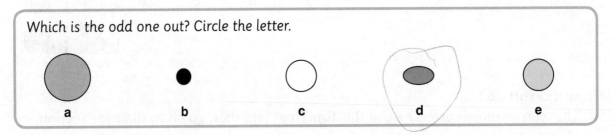

What immediately strikes you when you look at these options?

- They are all different sizes.
- They are all shaded differently.

So neither size nor shading can be the link here. Is there anything else about the shape of each option?

Starting from the left, let's look at each one in turn.

a is a circle   **b** is a circle   **c** is a circle   **d** is an oval   **e** is a circle

Four of the options are circles, so the odd one out must be **d** as it is a different **shape**.

Not all questions will use different-shaped options that can be seen quite quickly. Some links will be more subtle and you will need to look more closely to find the element they have in common.

Look at this next example.

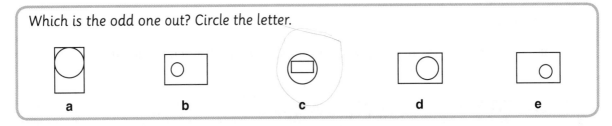

Unlike in the last example, each of these options is made up of the same shapes – a circle and a rectangle. Shape therefore cannot be the link here.

The circles and rectangles are different sizes in all of the symbols so you cannot use size to find the answer.

Look at each option, starting with **a**. How would you describe each one?

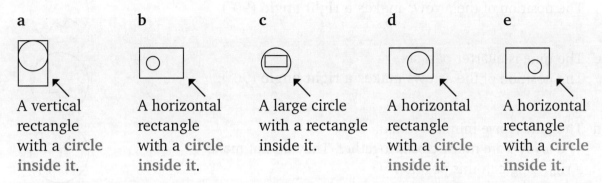

a — A vertical rectangle with a **circle** inside it.

b — A horizontal rectangle with a **circle** inside it.

c — A large circle with a rectangle inside it.

d — A horizontal rectangle with a **circle** inside it.

e — A horizontal rectangle with a **circle** inside it.

What do four of the shapes have in common? Shapes **a**, **b**, **d** and **e** are all made up of a rectangle with a circle inside. Option **c** shows the reverse. The **positions** of the circle and rectangle are different so this option must be the odd one out.

You may need to use your knowledge of maths to answer some non-verbal reasoning questions. Here are two examples of where your maths skills would help you to find the answer to similarities questions.

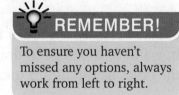

REMEMBER!

To ensure you haven't missed any options, always work from left to right.

Which is the odd one out? Circle the letter.

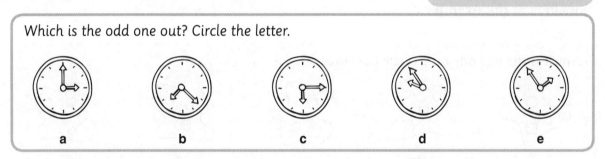

a b c d e

Each option shows the same circular clock face, so shape and size cannot be the link that will determine the answer. Look more closely at the symbols, what features make up each one?

Each symbol has:

- a small circle in the middle with two arrows connected to it
- 12 small lines that the arrows point towards
- two outer circles.

As they each have the same visible features, the link shared by four of the symbols must be something more subtle.

Although each option is made up of the same elements, they do all look different. Why? The clock faces are showing different times so the two arrows are in different positions in each shape. Look at each option in turn and describe what you can see.

a The time is three o'clock.
The position of the arrows **makes a right angle** (90°).

b The time is about 23 minutes past seven.
The position of the arrows **makes a right angle** (90°).

c The time is quarter past six.
The position of the arrows **makes a right angle** (90°).

d The time is five minutes to ten.
The arrows are much closer together. They do not make
a right angle in this position.

e The time is five minutes to two.
The position of the arrows **makes a right angle** (90°).

Looking closely at each of the options shows us that the arrows make right angles in **a**, **b**, **c** and **e**. You need to draw on your knowledge of **angles** in order to work out that the odd one out in this question is **d**.

Now look at this example.

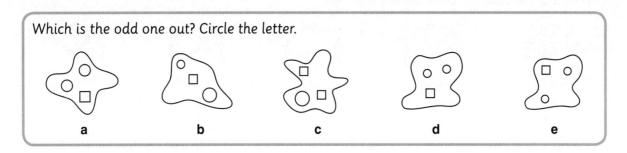

You can see quite quickly that:

- the outline of each shape is different
- each one contains circles and squares
- the position of the circles and squares is different in each option.

None of these elements will lead you to the answer.

So, starting with **a**, think about how you could describe each shape. It may help to draw a grid to note down what you can see.

Shape	Number of circles	Number of squares
a	2	1
b	2	1
c	1	2
d	2	1
e	2	1

It is clear from the information in the grid that the odd one out is **c**; it has one less circle and one more square than the other four shapes. The link here relates to **number**.

These last two examples of similarities question types test your observation skills rather than your knowledge of maths.

Let's look at the first example.

Which is the odd one out? Circle the letter.

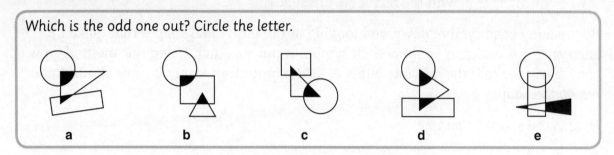

a   b   c   d   e

A quick look at each option shows that:

- each symbol is made up of a circle, a triangle and a rectangle
- the circle in each option is the same size
- the triangles and rectangles are all different sizes
- the circle, triangle and rectangle are in different positions in each option.

Shape, size and position can therefore be eliminated, as none of these elements can be the common feature between four of the symbols.

Look again at the symbols. How are the individual shapes connected in each one?

a

The area where the circle and triangle **overlap is shaded**.

The area where the triangle and rectangle **overlap is shaded**.

b

The area where the circle and rectangle **overlap is shaded**.

The area where the rectangle and triangle **overlap is shaded**.

c

The area where the rectangle and triangle **overlap is shaded**.

The area where the triangle and circle **overlap is shaded**.

d

The area where the circle and triangle **overlap is shaded**.

The area where the triangle and rectangle **overlap is shaded**.

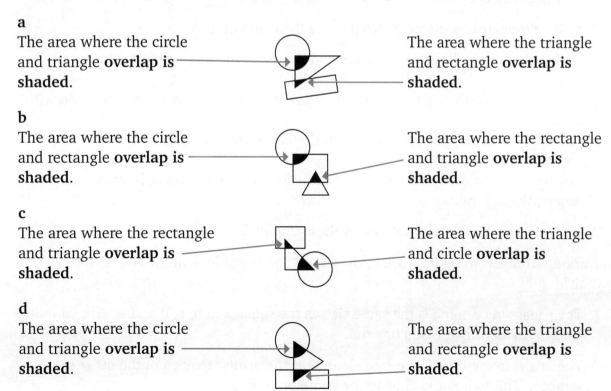

e

The area where the circle and rectangle **overlap is not shaded**.

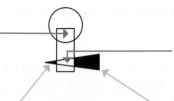

The area where the rectangle and triangle **overlap is not shaded**.

The parts of the triangle that do not overlap with the rectangle are shaded.

By breaking each symbol down and looking at the individual shapes that make up each one, it is easier to see how each symbol is put together. Using this method, you can clearly see that the odd one out is **e**, as the other four symbols have **shaded** areas where the shapes overlap.

Here is the second example.

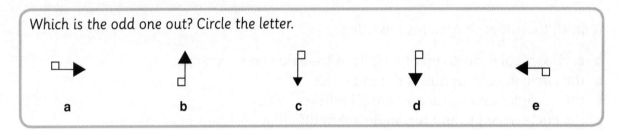

Which is the odd one out? Circle the letter.

a   b   c   d   e

Looking at these symbols quickly they all seem very similar. This means the feature that makes one stand out as being 'odd' to the other four options must be a very slight change. You must look at each option very carefully to find the common feature that four of the symbols share.

Can you eliminate any elements from being the common link?

- Each symbol is made up of an arrow and a square; the link cannot be to do with shape.
- Each arrow is shaded black and each square is white; the link cannot be to do with shading.
- The arrows are all pointing in different directions; the link cannot be to do with direction.
- The square is on the left-hand side of some arrows and on the right-hand side of others; the link cannot be to do with position.

What else could be different for one of these options?

Working from left to right, break each symbol down and look at the two shapes individually.

1 The square in option **a** is the same size as the squares in **b**, **c**, **d** and **e**. This cannot be used to identify the odd one out.

2 The arrow in option **a** is the same length as the arrows in each of the other symbols. This will not lead us to the common link.

3 The arrowhead in option **a** is:

- the same size as the arrowhead in **b**.   a →▶ ▲│ **b**

- larger than the arrowhead in **c**.   a →▶ │▼ **c**

- the same size as the arrowhead in **d**.   a →▶ ▼ **d**

- the same size as the arrowhead in **e**.   a ▶ ◀ **e**

Has a common feature been found that is shared by four of the options? Yes, the arrowheads in **a**, **b**, **d** and **e** are all the same **size**. Symbol **c** has a smaller arrowhead so this must be the odd one out.

You can see that in this example, there is a very subtle difference between the options. This can make questions more difficult to answer so you need to look at the detail of every option carefully and use your powers of observation.

Now it's your turn!

Which is the odd one out? Circle the letter.

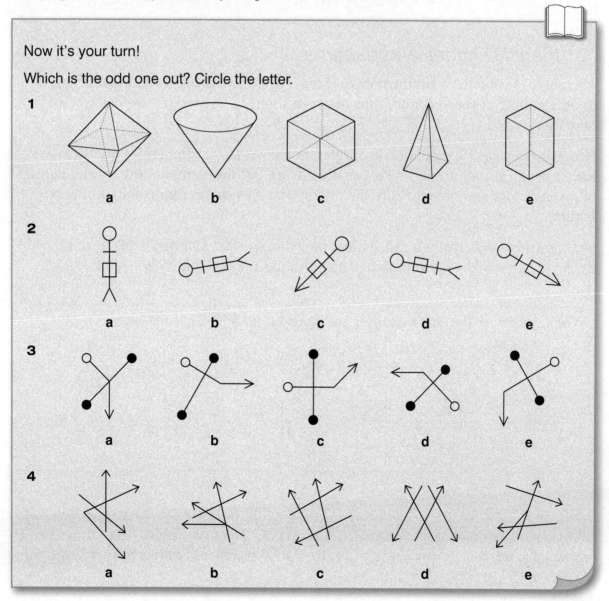

1   a   b   c   d   e

2   a   b   c   d   e

3   a   b   c   d   e

4   a   b   c   d   e

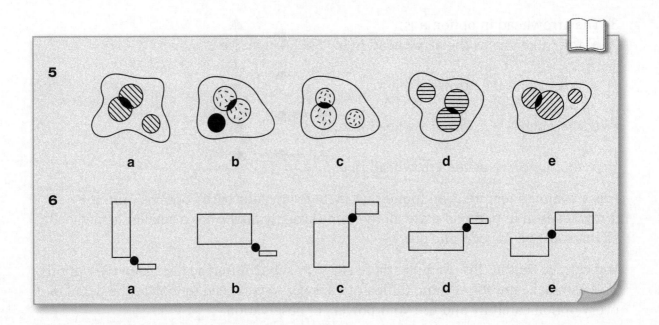

② Identify shapes and patterns

This set also contains a **similarities** question type, so your observation skills and understanding of visual connections between shapes and patterns are being tested here too.

However, this type is presented in a different format to the similarities questions we have already looked at. This time you must work out the common link within a group of given shapes and then identify the option that also shares that common link or feature.

We know now that symbols can share a range of possible features. Look at this example. It shows how a variety of common links may be combined.

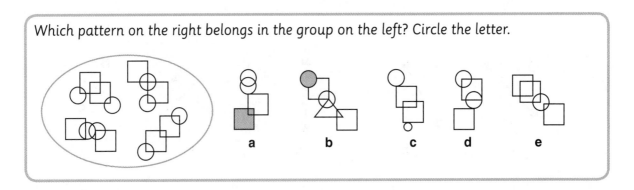

Which pattern on the right belongs in the group on the left? Circle the letter.

💡 REMEMBER!

Make sure you find all the connections in the given set – you need to find the option that shares all of these links.

Often, symbols can share more than one common link or feature. Look closely at the symbols in the given set in turn. What do you notice about each one?

1 Each symbol is made up of only 2 squares and 2 circles.
2 The squares and circles are the same size for all symbols.
3 The squares and circles are in different positions in each symbol.
4 None of the shapes are shaded.

Think about the conclusions you can draw about the correct option from your observations. Write a quick correct option checklist if it helps:

- Must have only 2 squares and 2 circles.
- Squares and circles must be the same size as in the given set.
- Squares and circles can be in any position.
- Shapes will have no shading.

To find the symbol that shares all of the features you have identified, you must now compare each option with the checklist you have put together. It can be helpful to draw a quick grid for this checking process. The correct option will have a ✓ next to each common link.

Common feature	a	b	c	d	e
Must have only 2 □ and 2 ○.	✓	✗	✓	✓	✗
□ and ○ must be the same size as in given set.	✓	—	✗	✓	—
□ and ○ can be in any position.	✓	—	—	✓	—
Shapes will have no shading.	✗	—	—	✓	—

It is clear from working through this checking process that option **d** must be the correct answer as it is the only option that shares each of the common features with the symbols in the given set.

REMEMBER!

Remember, symbols can be connected by a combination of any of these elements: size, position, angles, number, shape or shading.

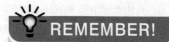
REMEMBER!

Cross out an option as soon as you have discounted it. This will help you to clearly see what's left.

Now it's your turn!

Which pattern on the right belongs in the group on the left? Circle the letter.

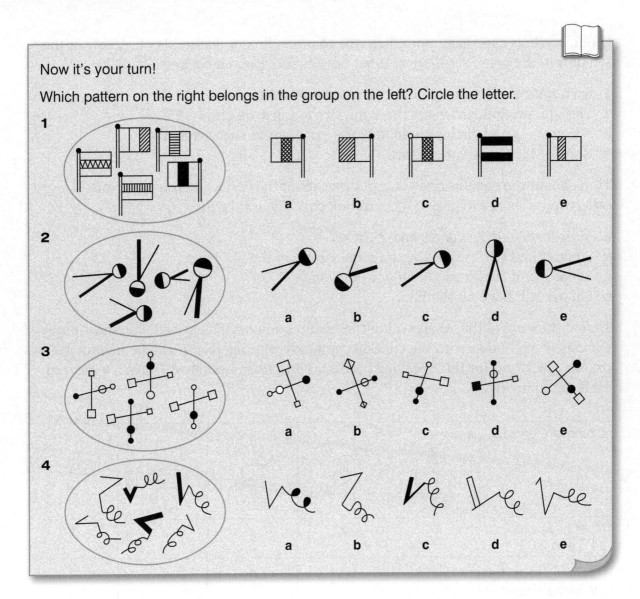

1

    a   b   c   d   e

2

    a   b   c   d   e

3

    a   b   c   d   e

4

    a   b   c   d   e

③ Pair up shapes

The question types that make up this set are called **analogies**. You may be familiar with this type of question from verbal reasoning tests. In both verbal and non-verbal reasoning, analogy questions test your ability to spot a connection between two concepts. You must then be able to apply this same relationship to something else.

The difference with the non-verbal reasoning type is that these questions involve **visual** analogies – you must identify the link between a pair of given pictures, shapes or patterns rather than words.

You will usually be given one pair of images that are connected in a particular way and the first image of a second pair. You have to find the correct image to complete the second pair in the same way as the first pair.

As with the similarities group, analogies can be based on a variety of different connections. Don't worry if you can't see a link straight away. You will find that some links will be easier to see than others.

Let's start with some of the more straightforward examples.

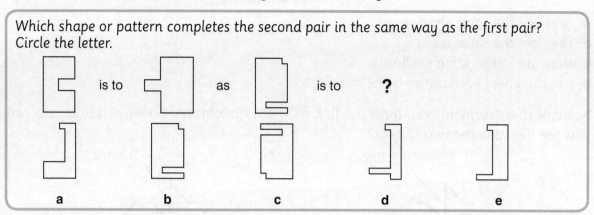

Which shape or pattern completes the second pair in the same way as the first pair? Circle the letter.

is to ... as ... is to **?**

a   b   c   d   e

1 Look carefully at the first pair of shapes. How would you describe them?

The first shape is a rectangle with a small piece missing from the centre.

The second shape is a rectangle with a small additional piece jutting out in the centre.

2 How might these two shapes be connected?

If both shapes were joined together, the second symbol would complete the first one to form one whole rectangle.

3 Now you have found the visual link that connects the first pair, apply this to the second pair.

Which option will make a complete rectangle when joined with the first shape of the second pair?

Work from left to right and compare the given shape with each option.

4 Following this careful checking process you will find that option **d** will make a complete rectangle when joined with the given shape.

This first example shows how analogies can be based on **shape**.
Now let's look at an example with a different type of connection.

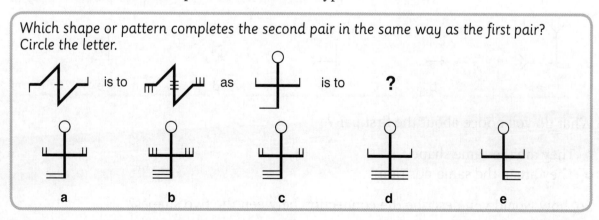

Which shape or pattern completes the second pair in the same way as the first pair? Circle the letter.

is to ... as ... is to **?**

a   b   c   d   e

A quick look at the first pair of objects shows that:

- they are the same shape
- they are the same size
- they are in the same position
- the thickness of the lines is the same.

None of these elements can form the link between the objects. So what differences can you see between the two shapes?

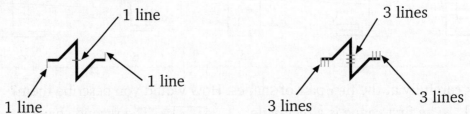

The connection between these two shapes is related to **number**; each short single line in the first symbol has become three short lines in the second symbol.

Now you can use this analogy to predict which symbol will complete the second pair.

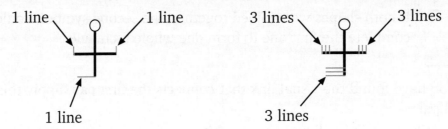

This predicted symbol matches option **b**, so this must be the answer.

This next version of an analogy question also uses a connection that can be quite simple to identify.

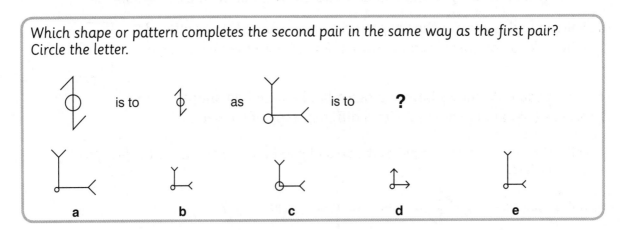

Which shape or pattern completes the second pair in the same way as the first pair? Circle the letter.

What do you notice about the first pair?

- They are the same shape.
- They are in the same position.

So, how would you describe the connection between the two shapes?

The second image is a smaller copy of the first one; the connection between these shapes relates to **size**. There is no other change so this rule can be applied easily to the second pair.

Work through each option and compare them with the given shape to find the answer. As before, it can be helpful to make brief notes about each option in a grid.

REMEMBER!

Check all options carefully to make sure you find the best answer.

Looking carefully at the options in this example, you should find that the correct answer is **b**: is to

---

✓ PARENT TIP

Improve your child's analysis and visual connection skills by setting them analogy style puzzles using everyday items. For example: place a 10 pence piece and 10 marbles on a table. Then put a 2 pence piece down and place a range of different items in groups on the other side of the table (such as two sweets, four marbles, six pencils, five cups, one 5 pence piece). Now explain that there is a link between the 10 pence piece and the 10 marbles and they need to find that link and use it to place the right item or items next to the 2 pence piece. In this example, the link is to do with number. A 10 pence piece is paired with 10 marbles, so the 2 pence piece would be paired with the two sweets. Try timing your child for each puzzle. It will help to make this game more challenging and exciting as they try to beat their previous time.

This next example shows another common link that is often used in visual analogy questions.

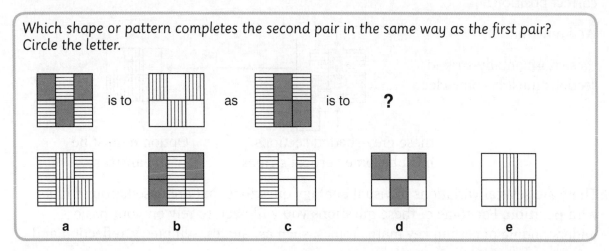

Which shape or pattern completes the second pair in the same way as the first pair? Circle the letter.

You should be able to see quite quickly that the connection for this analogy question relates to **shading**.

Before you look at exactly how the shading is different though, make sure that there are no other differences between the first pair. In this example, the objects are:

- the same shape
- the same size
- split into the same number of sections
- in the same position.

So, let's look more closely at the shading. How does the shading in the first shape change in the second shape?

1 These grey shaded sections have become vertical stripes.

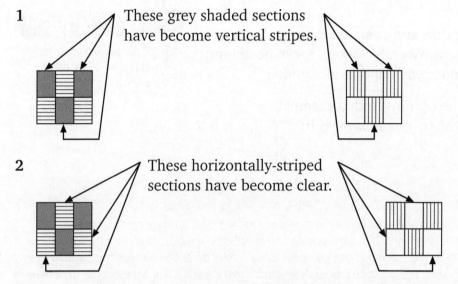

2 These horizontally-striped sections have become clear.

Now look at the first shape in the second pair. How will the shape change when these rules are applied?

You know that the correct option must have a combination of clear sections and striped sections. You can therefore discount options **a**, **b** and **d** straight away.

Compare options **c** and **e** with the given shape. Which one has the shading in the correct position?

We know that:

these horizontally-striped sections must become clear.

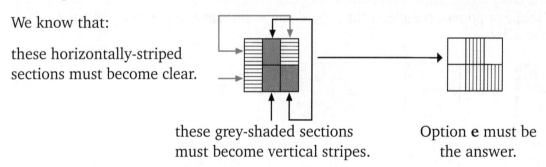

these grey-shaded sections must become vertical stripes.

Option **e** must be the answer.

There are several variations of visual analogy questions that are based around links with **position**. For some of these questions you will need to rely on your basic understanding of certain key maths topics, such as: angles, symmetry, reflection and rotation.

Let's look at some examples.

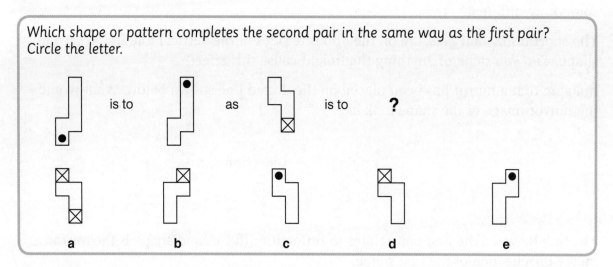

Which shape or pattern completes the second pair in the same way as the first pair? Circle the letter.

is to   as   is to   **?**

a   b   c   d   e

What do you notice about the first pair? Can you see the connection between the two shapes?

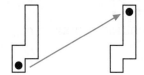

The shapes are identical except for the position of the shaded circle. It has moved from the bottom of the shape to the top.

This connection can now be applied to the second pair.

Remember to look closely at all the options. In this example, options **b** and **d** are very similar. The correct option must be **d** as it is the same shape as the given symbol.

The next two examples show more complex position changes. These may seem confusing at first but if you break the images down and look at them in sections it is easier to see what is going on.

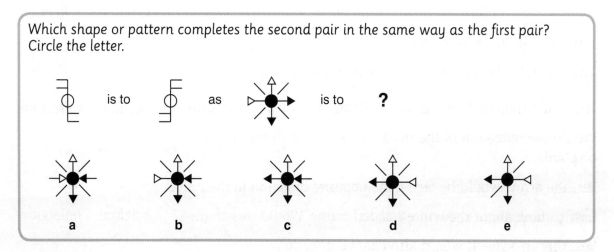

Which shape or pattern completes the second pair in the same way as the first pair? Circle the letter.

is to   as   is to   **?**

a   b   c   d   e

Compare the first pair of shapes. What do you notice?

The second shape is made up of the same lines and circle as the first one but there is something different.

The short horizontal lines are on the opposite sides of the vertical line in the second shape. Can you think of anything that might cause this effect?

Imagine that a mirror has been placed on the dotted line shown below. What would the mirror image of the shape look like?

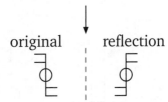

The link between the first pair relates to **reflection**; the second shape is the mirror image or reflection of the first shape.

This rule can now be applied to the second pair.

original   reflection

?

In this example, the first shape of the second pair has several elements so it may appear more difficult to work out.

For complex shapes like this, try to look at each section individually and think about how each one would be reflected in a mirror. This will help you to build up a full picture of the answer.

Here, you might start by thinking about the vertical arrows and the circle in the middle. What would they look like in a mirror?

The reflection of these shapes would look the same.

original   reflection

Next, you could look at the diagonal lines.

What would these look like?

These would also appear the same in a mirror.

original   reflection

You could then think about the horizontal arrows one at a time.

Would the reflection of the black arrow look different to the original?

Yes, the arrow would be facing the opposite direction in the reflection.

original   reflection

Lastly, think about the white-headed arrow. Would this change?

Yes, this arrowhead would also change direction.

original   reflection

Now that you have thought about how each part of the symbol would look in a mirror, you need to put all of the elements together to find the answer.

Which option shows the correct reflected image of the given shape in this example? _____

✓ **PARENT TIP**

Draw half a shape (such as a star or a kite) and ask your child to guess what the full shape would be. Then give him or her a mirror to place on the line of reflection to see if he or she guessed correctly. Or ask your child to complete the drawing before checking in the mirror.

☀ REMEMBER!

It can be helpful to draw a quick sketch of what you think the reflected shape will look like. You can then compare this with the options given.

Let's look at another example that may seem difficult to work out at first glance.

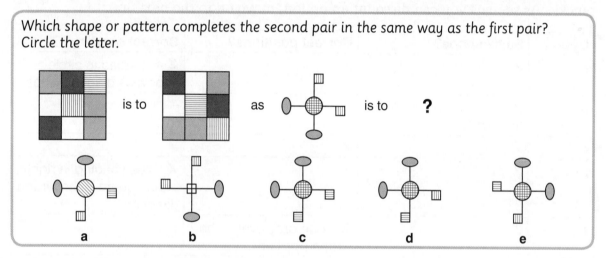

Which shape or pattern completes the second pair in the same way as the first pair? Circle the letter.

A quick look at the first pair of shapes shows that:

o they each have the same number of sections
o the same number of sections are patterned or shaded.

It is clear though that the shading has changed. Unlike in the example on page 19, the sections which have the same type of shading have not all been replaced with another type of shading. For example, the darker shaded section in the middle of the top row becomes white in the second shape, but the darker shaded section in the bottom left corner becomes light grey in the second shape, not white.

So what has made the shading appear different?

What would the first shape look like if you turned it?

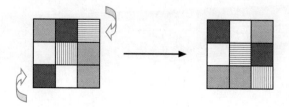

The position of the first shape has been changed; it has been **rotated** 90 degrees clockwise to form the second shape.

This rotation link can now be applied to complete the second pair.

REMEMBER!

Notice what happens to vertically and horizontally striped shading when it is rotated.

What would this shape look like if it was rotated 90 degrees clockwise?

Take one element at a time and think about what its new position would be once the shape is rotated.

Next, think about whether any of the shading will be affected by the rotation.

You may find it helpful to make brief notes so you can discount incorrect options quickly. As soon as you can discount an option, move on to the next one.

Option	Same shape?	Correct positions?	Correct shading?
a	✓	✓	✗ – shading in circle shown as diagonal lines
b	✗ – should be a circle in the middle	—	—
c	✓	✓	✓
d	✓	✓	✗ – line shading in right-hand square is the wrong direction
e	✓	✗ – one grey oval in the wrong position	—

From these notes we can deduce that the correct option in this example must be **c**.

REMEMBER!

Drawing a quick sketch can often help you to visualise a rotated shape. If you find this hard, try turning the paper round in the direction the shape needs to move.

PARENT TIP

Visualising a rotated shape can be one of the most difficult concepts for a child to grasp. Draw a shape and discuss with your child what it might look like if it was rotated by a range of different angles, e.g. 45°, 90°, 180° and 360°. Then use a piece of tracing paper to draw over the shape and rotate it around 360°. Were your predictions right?

Now it's your turn!

Which shape or pattern on the right completes the second pair in the same way as the first pair? Circle the letter.

1

    is to   as   is to

                              a   b   c   d   e

2

    is to   as   is to

                              a   b   c   d   e

3

    is to   as   is to

                              a   b   c   d   e

4

    is to   as   is to

                              a   b   c   d   e

5

    is to   as   is to

                              a   b   c   d   e

6

    is to   as   is to

                              a   b   c   d   e

- Symbols and patterns in many question types can be connected by a combination of **several different features or links**. Remember to check for:
  - **S**hape
  - **P**osition
  - **A**ngle
  - **N**umber
  - **S**hading
  - **S**ize

  Try using a **mnemonic** (a funny rhyme or story) to help you recall this list, for example:
  - **S**ean's **p**ets **a**re **n**aughty **s**aid **S**ally.
  - **S**potty **p**yjamas **a**nd **n**ice **s**oft **s**lippers!

- Symbols often have **more than one common feature**. Make sure you look at all the possibilities.

- If a symbol is made up of a number of parts, break it down and **look at one element at a time**. You should then find it easier to discount the incorrect options.

- Brush up on your **maths skills** – your knowledge of **angles, symmetry, reflection** and **rotation** will be especially useful when working out non-verbal reasoning questions.

- **Drawing a rough sketch** of your predicted answer can help you to visualise reflections and rotations. **Turning the paper round** can also be helpful when solving rotation questions.

- Making **notes in a grid** or writing a **correct option checklist** can be helpful when comparing a set of symbols.

- **Cross out incorrect options** as you discount them. This will make it easier to see what is left to choose from.

Missing shapes

This group of question types also tests your understanding of shape and pattern. It relies on your ability to:

- identify and apply a rule
- see shapes within shapes and patterns within patterns
- make deductions from given sets of objects or symbols.

Try this test to find out how many missing shapes question types you can already do. Circle the letter representing your chosen option for each question.

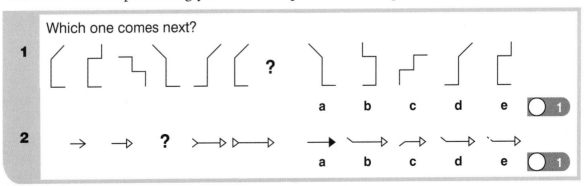

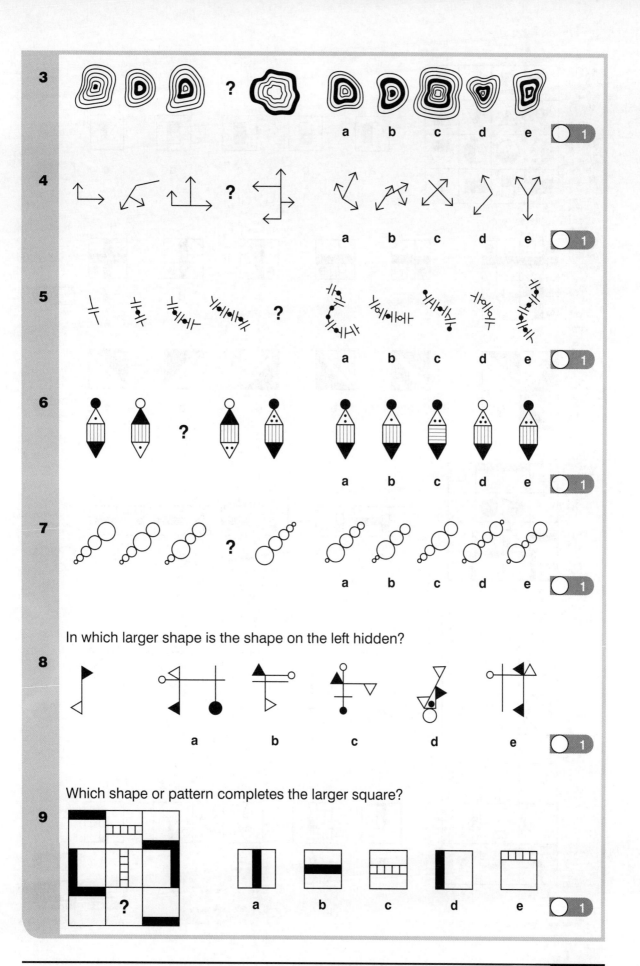

3

a b c d e

4

a b c d e

5

a b c d e

6

a b c d e

7

a b c d e

In which larger shape is the shape on the left hidden?

8

a b c d e

Which shape or pattern completes the larger square?

9

a b c d e

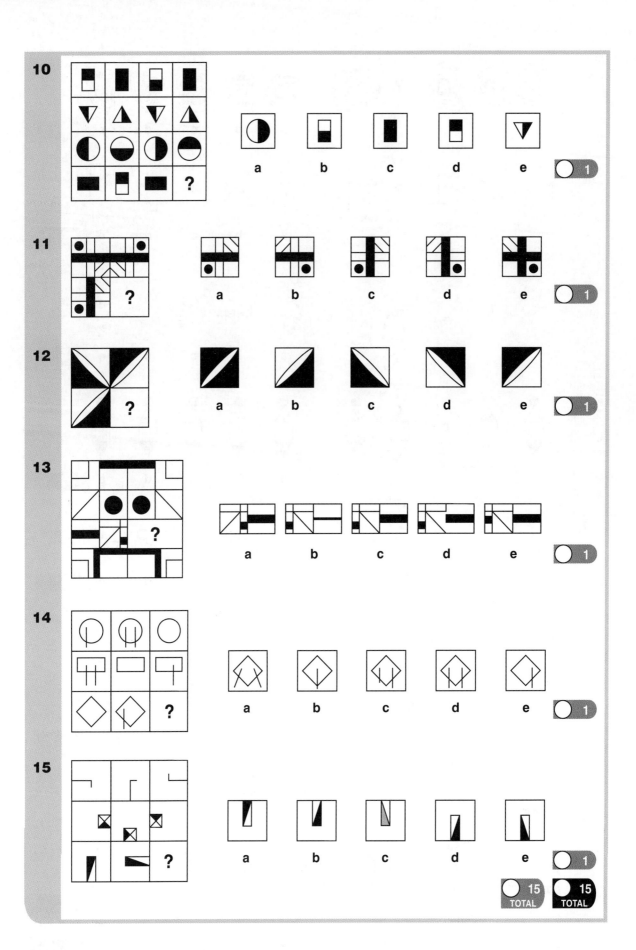

How to do ... 11+ Non-verbal Reasoning

How did you do?

- Thirteen or more correct? Read the **Top Tips!** and then go on to the next section: Rotating shapes.
- Twelve or fewer correct? Work through the question types in this section carefully and then retake the test!

When looking for the missing part of a larger pattern, what type of features should you think about? Let's look again at the spider diagram from the first section, Identifying shapes:

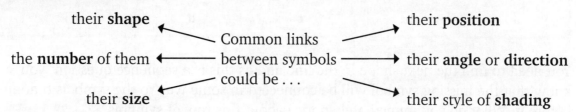

their **shape** → Common links ← their **position**

the **number** of them ← between symbols → their **angle** or **direction**

could be . . .

their **size** → their style of **shading**

As well as using these features to find common links and similarities, these elements can also help you to identify a missing shape or symbol. For example, a series or pattern of symbols may be based on:

- an increase or decrease in size or number
- alterations in shape, shading, position or direction.

There are three main sets of missing shapes questions. These are:

- Find shapes that complete a sequence.
- Find a given part within a shape.
- Find a missing shape from a pattern.

Let's work through this group of question types, looking at each one in turn.

> ### REMEMBER!
>
> A pattern or sequence may involve more than one element and different rules may have been applied to different features. Always look carefully and note down as many features as you can so that no aspect is overlooked or forgotten.

> ### ✔ PARENT TIP
>
> *Jigsaw puzzles are excellent practice for these question types, especially ones where the picture is quite complex, with a lot of detail.*

④ *Find shapes that complete a sequence*

The question types we will look at in this section are often referred to as **sequences** questions. They test your ability to identify and apply a given rule or rules in order to find the missing step in a sequence of images. You will need your observation and analysis skills to solve these question types.

Let's look at some examples, starting with one of the more straightforward sequences you may come across in a test paper.

Which one comes next? Circle the letter.

You need to find the next shape in the line and as this is a sequence question, you know that the missing symbol will be connected in some way to the symbols that are before it. What do you immediately notice about this row of symbols?

- They are all connected with music.
- They are all shaded black.
- They all appear upright and are similar in size.

So the type, shading, position and size of these symbols will not give any clues for working out the rule applied to this sequence.

Think about the first symbol (the treble clef) and look along the line. What do you notice? The treble clef reappears as the fifth symbol.

Now look at the second symbol (the 'natural sign'). As you look along the line you will see that this also reappears as the sixth symbol.

The symbols are being repeated; this is a **repeating pattern**. Now that the rule has been identified, it can easily be applied to find the symbol that comes next.

You know that the treble clef is the first and the fifth symbol. The treble clef must therefore start the repeating block. If it helps you to focus on the symbols, underline the repeating block.

Now match the pairs of symbols. Drawing arrows to link the pairs can help you see which symbol should come next.

Finally, look through the options and select the correct answer. In this example, the missing symbol is option **e**, the quaver.

This method can be used to solve any repeating sequence question, whether the sequence of images is made up of pictures, symbols, shapes or other patterns. Some answer options may be very similar, such as option **c** (the crotchet) and option **e** (the quaver) in this example. To make sure you choose the right answer, check all options very carefully.

In this first example the missing part of the sequence was at the end of the line of symbols. Not all sequence questions will follow this format. Here is an example where the missing link is within the sequence rather than at the end. You need to pay close attention to detail in this style of question.

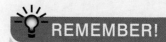

REMEMBER!

Repeating sequences are one of the easiest and quickest types of sequence questions to solve. Check for a repeating block first, before looking for any other rules and patterns in sequence questions.

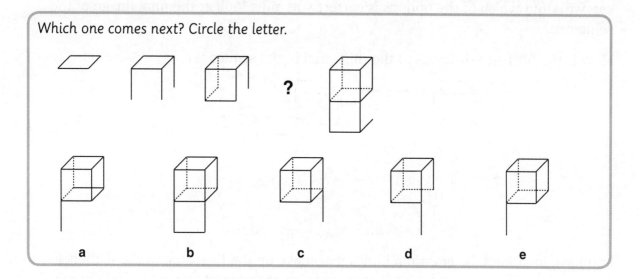

Which one comes next? Circle the letter.

?

a   b   c   d   e

You should be able to see quite quickly that this is not a repeating sequence. How would you describe what you can see?

- The steps in the sequence seem to be building a 3D shape.
- The shape grows larger at each stage.
- Some lines are dashed and some lines are solid.

How does the symbol change at each stage? Look at the first two steps. How is the **shape** different in the second step to the first step?

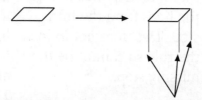

3 lines have been added

Now compare the second and third steps. How has the shape changed at the third step?

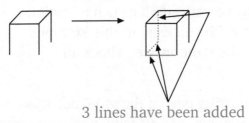

3 lines have been added

Has a common rule been found for the first three steps of this sequence? Yes, three lines have been added at each step in the sequence.

The fourth step in the sequence is the missing link you need to find but you know now that it must be made up of the third step plus three more lines. However, before you can work out which of the options is correct you must look at the final image of the sequence.

How is the fifth step different to the third step in the sequence?

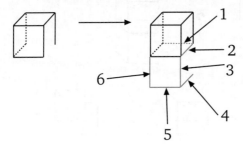

6 lines have been added

You have identified the additional lines that make up the final step in the sequence. Now you can look for the option that is made up of the third step, plus three of the lines that the fifth step contains.

Option **a** is made up of the third step plus three of the lines from the fifth step. But are the lines exactly the same? No. Look at the line the arrow is pointing to. In the fifth step this is a dashed line not a solid one. This cannot be the missing step.

Option **b** is made up of the third step plus five of the lines from the fifth step. This does not follow the rule so cannot be the missing step.

Option **c** is made up of the third step plus three more lines. But are all of these lines present in the fifth step? No. Look at the line the arrow is pointing to. This is not drawn in the fifth step of the sequence. This cannot be the missing step.

Option **d** is made up of the third step but it only has two of the lines from the fifth step. This cannot be the missing step.

Option **e** is made up of the third step plus three of the lines from the fifth step. This is the missing step.

It can be quite difficult to find the right option in sequences where the missing step is not at the end of the sequence. If you break the sequence down into steps and compare each step with the next one, it will make it easier to find the rule. Following a methodical and careful approach like the one shown here will ensure you find the missing symbol, wherever it is placed in the sequence.

The last example showed how changes to **shape** can form the link in a sequence. The next example looks at another common linking feature which requires your observation skills.

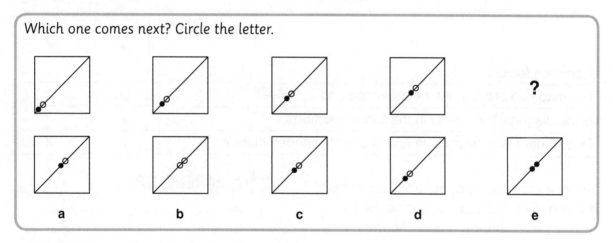

Which one comes next? Circle the letter.

a   b   c   d   e

What are the first points that come to mind when you look at this sequence of images?

Each picture is the same size and is made up of:

- a square
- a diagonal line pointing in the same direction
- one clear circle and one circle shaded black.

None of these elements will help you to find the image that comes next. What else can you see?

- Both of the circles are on the diagonal line.
- The clear circle is always above the black circle.
- The position of the circles changes in each step.

This last observation highlights a difference from one step of the sequence to the next. How does the **position** of the pair of circles change?

As the sequence progresses, the two circles move together along the diagonal line towards the top right-hand corner of the square. You can now use this rule to work out which image should come next.

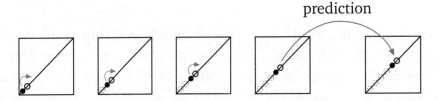

prediction

The circles were halfway along the line in the last given step. They will therefore need to be above the halfway position in the final step of this sequence.

First, use this rule to eliminate any options where the circles are not above the halfway point. This will make it faster to identify the answer. Following this process leaves options **a** and **b**.

Now compare these options with the common features you noted when you first looked at the sequence. You might find it helpful to use a grid for this.

Common feature	Option 	
Is it made up of a square, diagonal line and 2 circles?	✓	✓
Is the diagonal line runing in the same direction?	✓	✓
Does it have one clear circle and one circle shaded black?	✓	✗

You can stop the comparison here; option **b** has two clear circles so cannot be the missing step. Option **a** must be the correct answer.

This next example shows how you can use your maths knowledge to help work out the connection and rule for some sequence questions.

✓ **PARENT TIP**

Children may identify a correct option quickly and therefore not want to follow the suggested strategy in full to work out an 'easy' question. This is fine, but to ensure that they understand the method, ask them to explain the rule and justify their answer. Alternatively, select one of the wrong options and ask them to explain why that option is incorrect.

Which one comes next? Circle the letter.

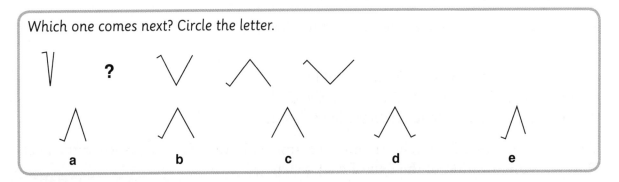

First, think about the features that each of the symbols share:

- they are all V-shaped
- they are all made up of three lines; one short line and two longer lines
- the short lines are all the same length
- the longer pairs of lines are all the same length
- the short line is always in front of the longer lines.

Now look at the symbols again. What makes each step of the sequence different to the next one? As you need to find the second step in this sequence, it is easier to look at the changes that occur between the last three consecutive symbols first.

1 The **angle** between the two longer lines increases with each step.

2 The **direction** of the V-shape alternates, pointing down then up.

3 The **direction** of the short line alternates, pointing down then up.

Keeping these differences in mind, you can now draw some conclusions about the missing symbol:

- It must have an angle greater than the first step and less than the third step.
- The direction of the V-shape must point upwards.
- The direction of the short line must point upwards.

You can now combine the checklist of common features with these conclusions and compare them with each option to identify the answer. As before, it can be helpful to make notes in a grid.

Following this process, you will find that option **a** is the correct answer to this example.

So far we have looked at how rules relating to repetition, shape, position, angle and direction can all form the basis of a sequence. This next example shows a simple version of another common feature that can be used in many different ways to create sequence questions.

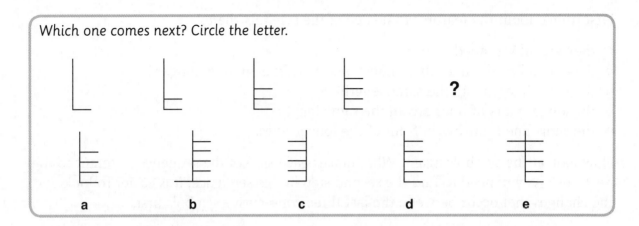

Which one comes next? Circle the letter.

a   b   c   d   e

In this sequence it is clear that:

- Each symbol has one vertical line and some horizontal lines.
- The vertical line is the same length in each symbol.
- The horizontal lines are the same length in each symbol.
- All the horizontal lines point to the right.

It seems easy to see then, that the only difference relates to the **number** of horizontal lines in each step of the sequence.

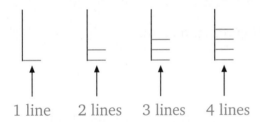

1 line   2 lines   3 lines   4 lines

The number of horizontal lines increases by one in each step of the sequence.

Now compare the answer options with this rule and the common features listed above. Options **b**, **c** and **e** can be eliminated quickly, as they have horizontal lines pointing to the left.

This leaves option **a**:   and option **d**:

The last step in the given sequence has four horizontal lines. As the number of lines increases by one each time, the next step must have five lines. Option **d** is therefore the correct answer.

The next example is based on another element that you may find at the root of many sequence questions. It is often quite easy to see changes to this feature but be careful, it may not be the only rule that applies in a sequence!

REMEMBER!

With questions that look very simple, it is easy to make a careless mistake. For instance, if you glance at the answer options too quickly in this example, you could choose option **c** just because it has five horizontal lines, without thinking about direction. Remember that answer options often have very subtle differences, so look very carefully at all elements!

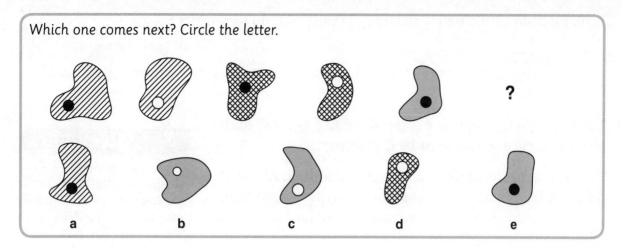

Which one comes next? Circle the letter.

a   b   c   d   e

As for the other types of sequence questions, think about what first strikes you about these symbols:

- Each symbol is a different shape and size.
- Each large shape is shaded in some way.
- Each large shape has a circle inside it.
- Each circle is the same size.

Now look at how each step compares with the next:

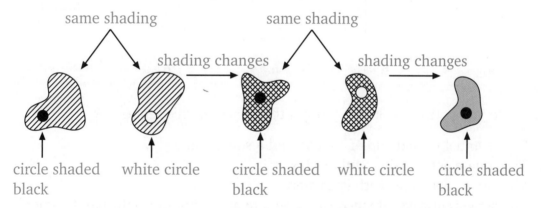

The rule behind this sequence is clearly related to **shading** and seems to have two aspects:

1 The shading of the large shape is grouped in pairs; the first and second symbols have the same background shading; the third and fourth share the same background shading and so on.

2 The shading of the small inner circle alternates between steps, changing from black to white.

Based on these points, it is possible to conclude that the next symbol in the sequence must:

- have a solid dark grey background – this eliminates options **a** and **d**
- contain a white circle – this eliminates option **e**.

Look carefully at the two remaining options; how do they differ?

The white circles are different sizes.

The inner circle in option **c** is the same size as those in the given sequence so this must be the answer.

Here is the last example of a sequence question. Although a different feature forms the base for this type of sequence, you can use the same strategies and techniques to find the missing step.

REMEMBER!

If you have trouble working out the links in a question, try to recall your mnemonic for SPANSS! See the Top Tips! section for suggestions.

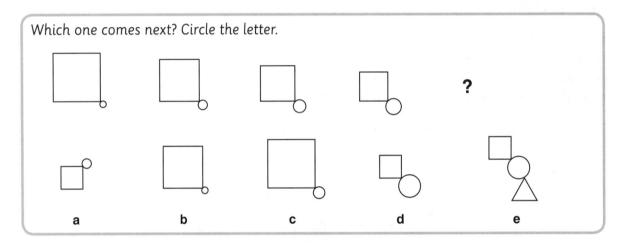

Which one comes next? Circle the letter.

a   b   c   d   e

What do you notice about the symbols that make up this sequence?

- Each symbol is made up of a circle and a square only.
- The square gets smaller with each step.
- The circle gets larger with each step.
- The circle is always attached to the square at the bottom right-hand corner.
- There is no shading.

You can now use these observations to make a quick correct option checklist.

The next symbol must have:

- a square smaller than in the fourth step
- a circle larger than in the fourth step
- a circle at the bottom right-hand corner of the square
- no shading
- no other shapes present.

Look at the answer options given. None of them contain any shading so you can now compare each of the options against the remaining four points on the correct option checklist:

Option	Smaller square?	Larger circle?	Circle at bottom right-hand corner?	No other shapes?
a	✓	✗	—	—
b	✗	—	—	—
c	✗	—	—	—
d	✓	✓	✓	✓
e	✓	✓	✓	✗

From the grid, it is clear that there is only one option that matches all of the elements. Option **d** must be the next step in the sequence.

REMEMBER!

As soon as you can eliminate an option, cross it out and move on.

Now it's your turn!

Which one comes next?

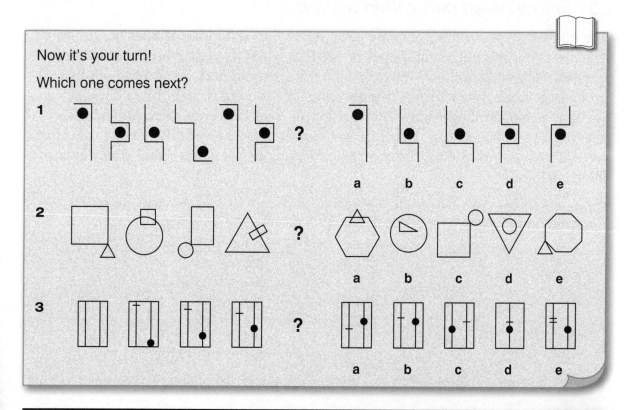

B: The key non-verbal reasoning question types   **39**

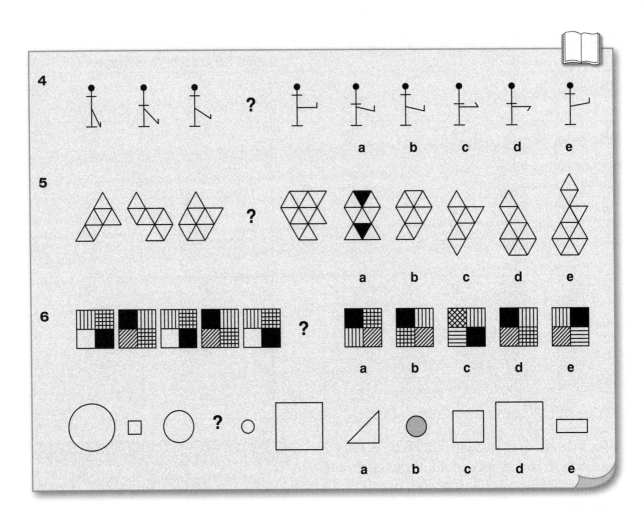

⑤ Find a given part within a shape

The question types in this group are often referred to as **hidden shapes** questions. They test your recognition of shapes or patterns when they are placed within larger symbols. As you do not have to work out a rule or try to find the odd one out in a group of symbols, you may feel this question type is quite straightforward. Some versions of hidden shapes questions can appear easy. However, elements such as shading or a complex shape structure can make this type more difficult to solve. Here we will look at two examples, one straightforward and one that may initially appear more complex.

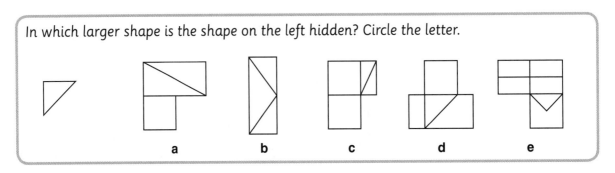

In which larger shape is the shape on the left hidden? Circle the letter.

First, make sure you know what you are looking for. In this example, you need to find:

Practice Test

11⁺ Non-verbal Reasoning

Read the instructions carefully.

- Do not begin the test or open the booklet until told to do so.

- Work as quickly and as carefully as you can.

- Circle the correct letter from the options given to answer each question.

- You may do rough working on a separate sheet of paper.

- If you make a mistake rub it out and circle the new answer clearly.

- You will have 30 minutes to complete the test.

Text © Alison Primrose, 2007

The right of Alison Primrose to be identified as author of this work has been asserted by her in accordance with the Copyright, Designs and Patents Act 1988.

All rights reserved. No part of this publication may be reproduced or transmitted in any form or by any means, electronic or mechanical, including photocopying, recording or any information storage and retrieval system, without permission in writing from the publisher or under licence from the Copyright Licensing Agency Ltd, of Saffron House, 6–10 Kirby Street, London, EC1N 8TS.

Any person who commits any unauthorised act in relation to this publication may be liable to criminal prosecution and civil claims for damages.

First published in 2002 by:
Nelson Thornes Ltd

This edition published 2007 by:
Nelson Thornes Ltd, Delta Place, 27 Bath Road
CHELTENHAM GL53 7TH, United Kingdom

A catalogue record for this book is available from the British Library

ISBN 978 0 7487 8121 8

Page make-up by Wearset Ltd

Published by Nelson Thornes. Nelson Thornes is an Infinitas Learning company, and is not associated in any way with NFER-Nelson.

Section 1

Which is the odd one out? Circle the letter.

1

   a   b   c   d   e

2

   a   b   c   d   e

3

   a   b   c   d   e

4

   a   b   c   d   e

Which pattern on the right belongs in the group on the left? Circle the letter.

5

   a   b   c   d   e

6

   a   b   c   d   e

7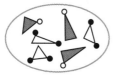

   a   b   c   d   e

8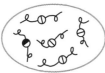

   a   b   c   d   e

9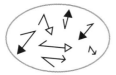

   a   b   c   d   e

10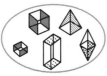

   a   b   c   d   e

1
1
1
1
1
1
1
1
1
1

10
TOTAL

Section 2

Which one comes next? Circle the letter.

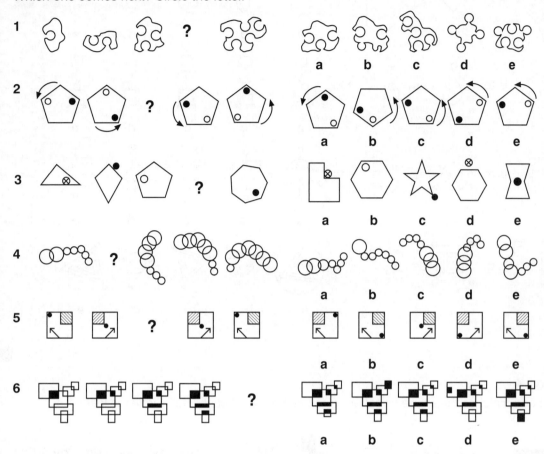

Section 3

Which shape or pattern on the right completes the second pair in the same way as the first pair? Circle the letter.

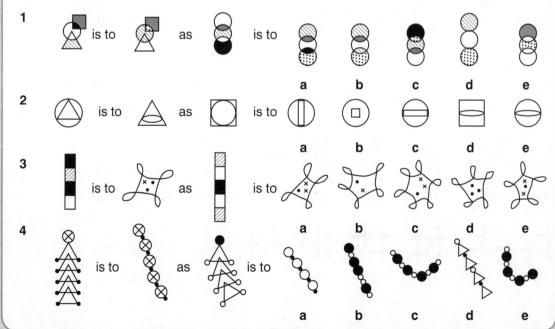

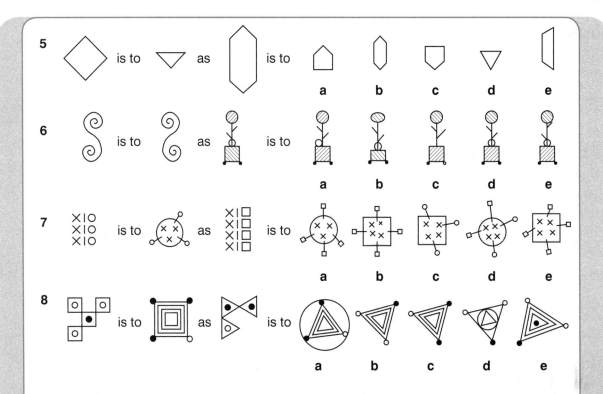

5 is to ... as ... is to

a b c d e

6 is to ... as ... is to

a b c d e

7 is to ... as ... is to

a b c d e

8 is to ... as ... is to

a b c d e

8 TOTAL

Section 4
Which code matches the shape or pattern given at the end of each line? Circle the letter.

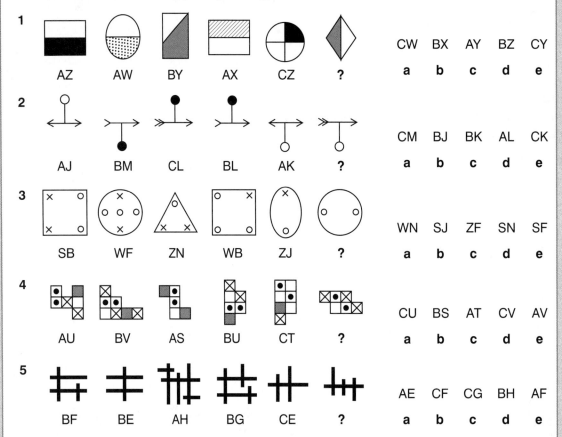

1

AZ · AW · BY · AX · CZ · ?

CW	BX	AY	BZ	CY
a	b	c	d	e

2

AJ · BM · CL · BL · AK · ?

CM	BJ	BK	AL	CK
a	b	c	d	e

3

SB · WF · ZN · WB · ZJ · ?

WN	SJ	ZF	SN	SF
a	b	c	d	e

4

AU · BV · AS · BU · CT · ?

CU	BS	AT	CV	AV
a	b	c	d	e

5

BF · BE · AH · BG · CE · ?

AE	CF	CG	BH	AF
a	b	c	d	e

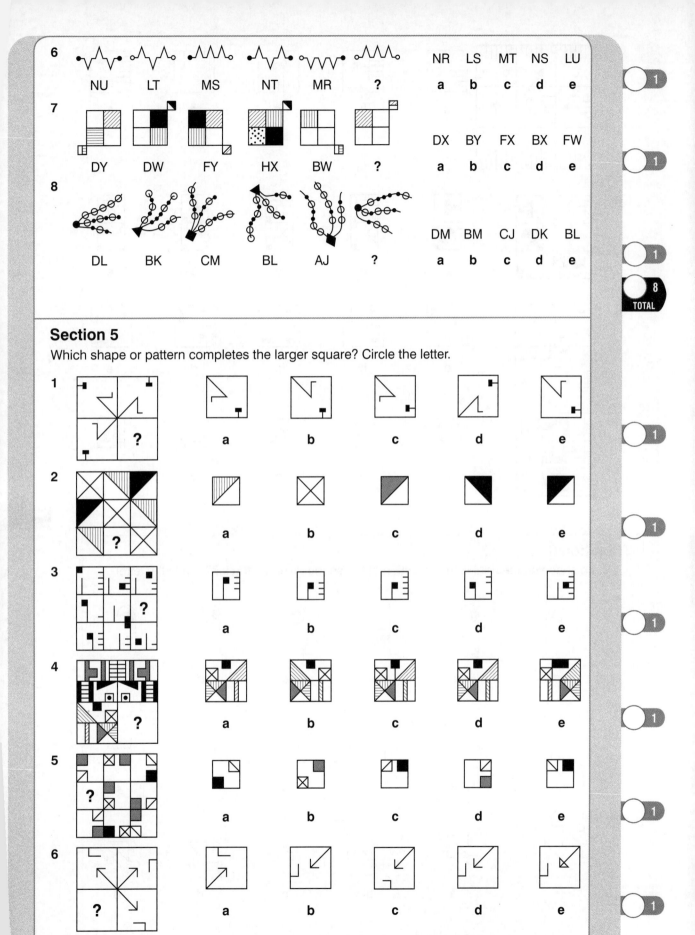

6

NR	LS	MT	NS	LU
a	b	c	d	e

NU   LT   MS   NT   MR   ?

7

DX	BY	FX	BX	FW
a	b	c	d	e

DY   DW   FY   HX   BW   ?

8

DM	BM	CJ	DK	BL
a	b	c	d	e

DL   BK   CM   BL   AJ   ?

8 TOTAL

Section 5

Which shape or pattern completes the larger square? Circle the letter.

1   a   b   c   d   e

2   a   b   c   d   e

3   a   b   c   d   e

4   a   b   c   d   e

5   a   b   c   d   e

6   a   b   c   d   e

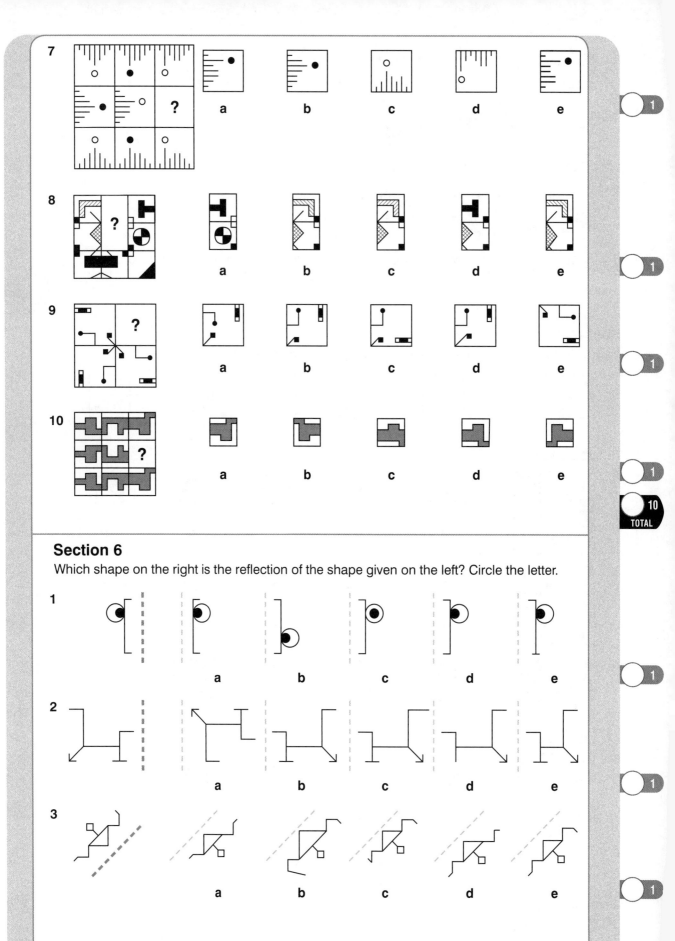

7

a b c d e

8

a b c d e

9

a b c d e

10

a b c d e

10 TOTAL

Section 6

Which shape on the right is the reflection of the shape given on the left? Circle the letter.

1

a b c d e

2

a b c d e

3

a b c d e

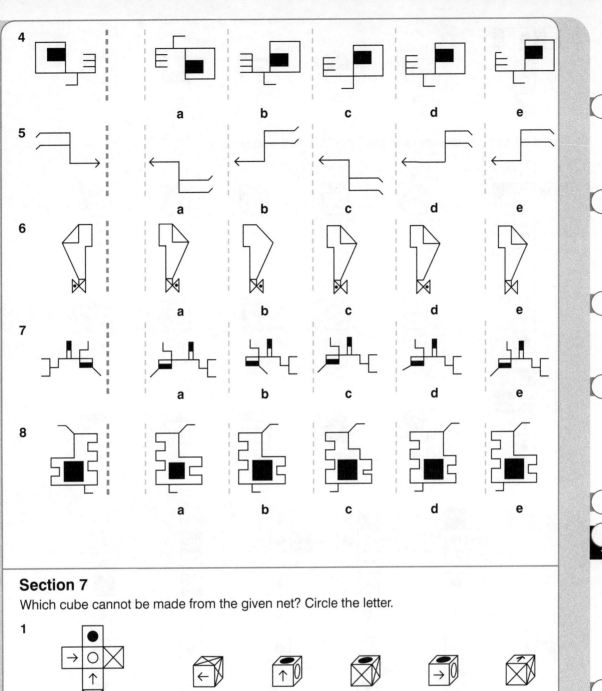

4 a b c d e

5 a b c d e

6 a b c d e

7 a b c d e

8 a b c d e

Section 7

Which cube cannot be made from the given net? Circle the letter.

1 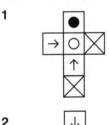 a b c d e

2 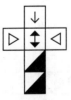 a b c d e

3   a b c d e

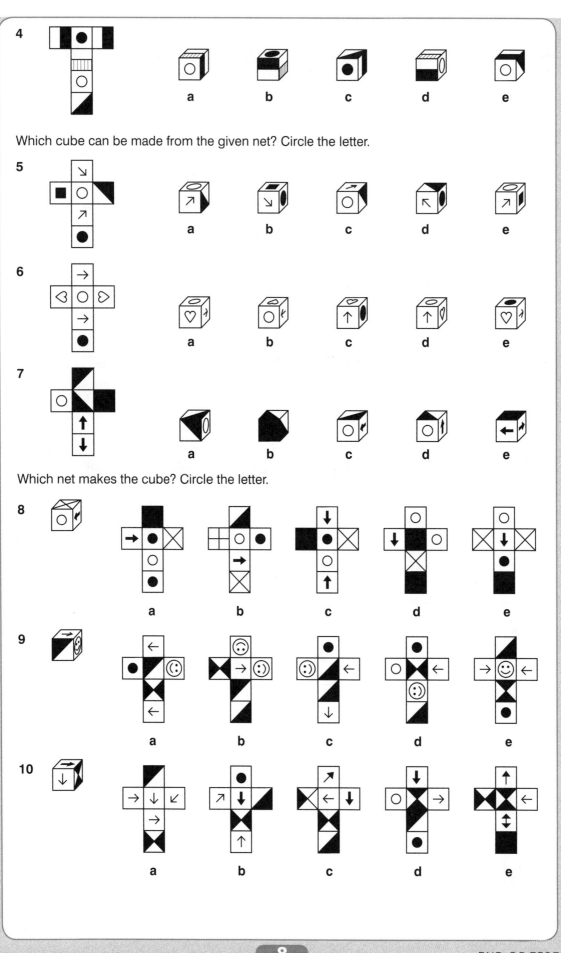

4

Which cube can be made from the given net? Circle the letter.

5

6

7

Which net makes the cube? Circle the letter.

8

9

10

END OF TEST

a small right-angled triangle with two sides of equal length.

Now, examine each of the options in turn and highlight any triangles within the symbols.

Which options contain a right-angled triangle with two sides of equal length? Options **d** and **e**.

Now compare these two right-angled triangles. Are they the same as the given triangle?

Remember, you must find an exact match in size, shape, shading, angle etc.

Given
triangle: Triangle in
option **d**:   Triangle in
option **e**:

It is now easy to see that option **d** has the given triangle hidden in its structure.

> ✔ **PARENT TIP**
>
> *When practising this question type, it can help to cut out the given shape and then physically test it against the answer options. If this is done with paper that is coloured on one side it can be used to show how the flip-side of the shape will appear differently. Or, trace over the given shape and place it over each option in turn.*

Now let's look at an example that may not be so easy to see.

> In which larger shape is the shape on the left hidden? Circle the letter.
>
> **a**   **b**   **c**   **d**   **e**

As the given shape and all of the options here have shaded areas, it is more difficult to locate the shape straight away. One of the most effective strategies for this type of hidden shape question is to break the given shape down into smaller chunks and look closely at how it is constructed:

2 black squares of equal size; each one quarter of the size of white square

black squares on adjacent edges of white square

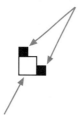

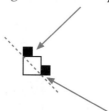

1 large white square

black squares attached to diagonally opposite corners of white square

Now follow a methodical approach, looking for these elements in the given options one at a time.

First, look for all of the large white squares in the options.

Then highlight any that have two small black squares attached at corners.

Option **b** contains three large white squares and option **d** has two large white squares but none of these have two black squares attached at corners. These options can therefore be discounted.

This leaves:

Option **a**

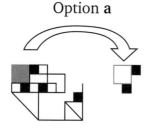

Option **c**

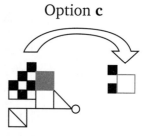

You may be able to see another four large white squares in this pattern but none of these squares have two black squares attached.

There are two further large white squares here but these do not have two black squares attached at the corners.

Option **e**

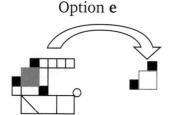

There is one more large square in this pattern but it is not attached to any black squares.

Which of these hidden shapes matches the given shape?

Given shape   Option **a**   Option **c**   Option **e**

Again, making notes in a grid about the correct option criteria can be useful here.

Criteria	Option a	Option c	Option e
1 large white square	✓	✓	✓
2 black squares of equal size; each one quarter of the size of white square	✓	✓	✓
Black squares on adjacent edges of white square	✓	✗	✓
Black squares attached to diagonally opposite corners of white square	✗	—	✓

From the notes in the grid it seems that option **e** must be the answer, but it looks different to the given shape. If you are unsure if a symbol is the same, think about what the given shape would look like if it were rotated.

This is how the given shape in this example would look rotated around 360 degrees:

Option **e** is the same as the given shape, rotated 270 degrees clockwise (or 90 degrees anticlockwise). It is therefore the correct answer.

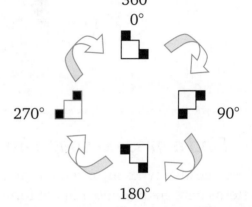

✔ **PARENT TIP**

Picture puzzles where you have to look for hidden objects, such as the range of Where's Wally *books or spot-the-difference games, are excellent practice for hidden shapes question types.*

💡 **REMEMBER!**

Other shapes may overlap the hidden shape. The given shape may be in a different direction once it's hidden.

Now it's your turn!

In which larger shape is the shape on the left hidden? Circle the letter.

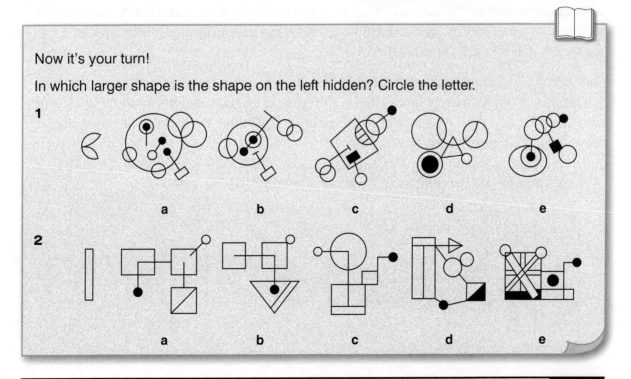

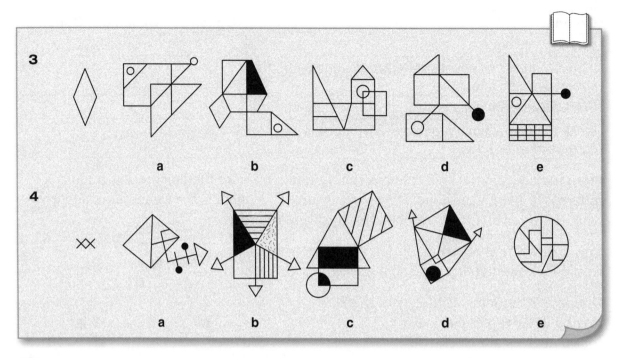

⑥ Find a missing shape from a pattern

These question types are often referred to as **matrix** (or matrices) questions as the patterns here are presented in the form of a grid. They may seem more complex as, unlike in other non-verbal reasoning questions, the patterns or symbols in matrices are not shown in a straight line.

However, a matrix question is usually based on one or more of the links we have already explored in relation to similarities, analogies and sequences. Some, such as those based on repetition, may be quite straightforward to see, while other patterns, such as those formed by rotation, may be more difficult. If you approach each matrix question in a methodical and careful way, breaking each grid down into smaller chunks, it will be easier to find the rule.

The following examples show four of the most common rules that a matrix question can be based on. As matrix grids can be different sizes, two examples show grids with nine sections and two use grids of four sections. Let's start by looking at one of the most straightforward versions of matrices.

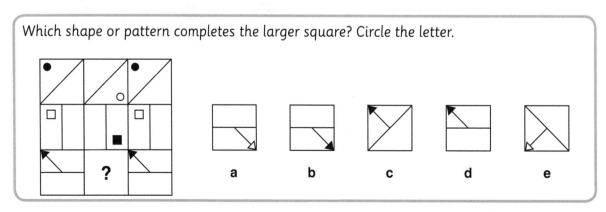

Which shape or pattern completes the larger square? Circle the letter.

Are there any general things that strike you about the grid?

- The grid has three rows and three columns.
- Each row looks different.
- The first and the third columns look the same.
- There are nine squares.
- Each square contains a line and another symbol.
- Each square is divided in half.

None of these observations will immediately help you to identify the missing square, so now break the grid down into chunks.

Look at the top row. There are four features here.

1 Each square is divided in half by a diagonal line.

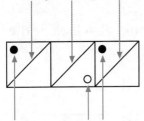

2 Each square contains a small circle.

3 The position of the circle changes.

top left corner   bottom right corner   top left corner

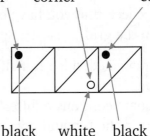

black   white   black

4 The colour of the circle alternates.

Now look at the given squares in the remaining two rows. Do they have anything in common with the features found in the top row? You may find it helpful to make brief notes in a grid.

	Top row	Middle row	Bottom row
Each square is divided in half by a:	diagonal line	vertical line	horizontal line
Each square contains:	a small circle	a small square	an arrow
Position of small symbol moves from:	top left – bottom right – top left	top left – bottom right – top left	top left – ? – top left
Colour of small symbol alternates from:	black – white – black	white – black – white	black – ? – black

Breaking down the matrix into rows has shown that a **repeating pattern** is forming based on elements of shape, shading and position. We can now use these notes to predict what the missing square in the bottom row will look like.

According to the first two rules indicated above, the missing square must:

- be divided in half by a horizontal line
- contain an arrow.

The third point in the grid shows that the small symbols in the top and middle rows follow the same pattern of movement. The position of the arrow in the two given squares also suggests that the bottom row follows the same alternating pattern. This means that the arrow in the missing square will point to the bottom right corner.

The colour of the small symbols also changes. Looking at the notes in the grid, it is clear that the pattern is alternating from black to white. To complete this pattern, the arrow in the missing square must be white.

Now that you have identified the four factors that the missing square must contain, it is easy to look at each of the options and find the correct answer. You can compare the options in a grid if it will help you to focus on the four elements that the answer must have.

Following this methodical process, you should find that option **a** meets all of the criteria in this example.

To double check that you have chosen the correct option, you could also look at the columns in the grid.

1 Each square is divided in half in a different direction.
2 Each square contains a different symbol.
3 Symbols in the top and bottom squares are the same colour.
4 All symbols are placed in (or point towards) the same corner.

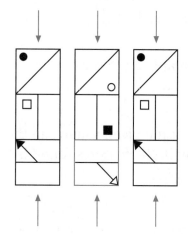

> ☀ **REMEMBER!**
>
> If you cannot see a pattern in each row, try looking at the features in each column. The rule may apply to the columns rather than the rows.

Now let's look at another example based on a rule that can also be quite easy to spot.

Which shape or pattern completes the larger square? Circle the letter.

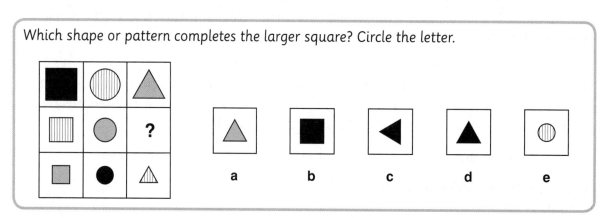

You may be able to see the rule in this type of matrix question straight away, but don't worry if you can't. Follow the same process as before, breaking the matrix down into chunks and looking at it in individual sections.

So for this example, you could first look at each column and describe what you see. Start with the left column:

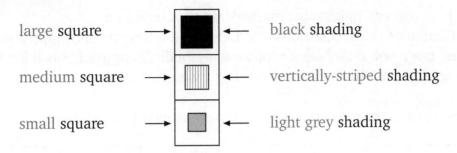

large square → black shading

medium square → vertically-striped shading

small square → light grey shading

Is a pattern forming? Yes! The first column shows that:

- all boxes show the same symbol
- the symbol decreases in size from the top to the bottom
- each symbol is shaded differently.

Now compare these features with the second column. Does it also follow these rules? Yes, each box shows a circle; the circles decrease in size; each circle is shaded differently.

This confirms that the rule here must be a **sequence** based on size and shading. It should now be quite straightforward to identify the missing symbol. Remember, making notes in a grid can help you to find the answer quickly.

	Left column	Middle column	Right column
All boxes shown contain a:	square	circle	triangle
Size of top symbol	large	large	large
Size of middle symbol	medium	medium	?
Size of bottom symbol	small	small	small
Colour of top symbol	black	vertical stripes	light grey
Colour of middle symbol	vertical stripes	light grey	?
Colour of bottom symbol	light grey	black	vertical stripes

From these notes, can you see why the missing square of the matrix will contain a **black, medium-sized triangle?** Each column has:

- the same shaped symbol in each box – the missing box in the right-hand column must contain a triangle
- a large, medium and small version of the symbol – the right-hand column is missing a medium-sized symbol
- one example of each type of shading – the right-hand column is missing a black symbol.

These criteria mean that options **a**, **b** and **e** can be eliminated.

REMEMBER!

To check that you have chosen the right option, also look at the pattern in each row.

Both options **c** and **d** show medium-sized black triangles but they look different. Option **d** must be the answer as it is pointing in the same direction as the other two triangles in the matrix.

The next two examples show matrices that are based on more complex rules. Questions that follow these formats may appear more confusing at first but if you remember to follow a methodical approach, breaking the grid down into sections, it will be easier to work out what is happening.

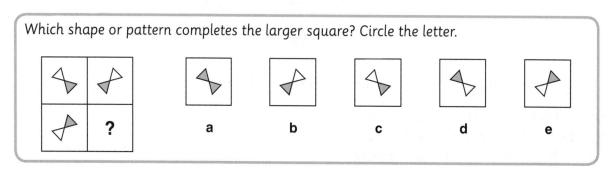

Which shape or pattern completes the larger square? Circle the letter.

a   b   c   d   e

It should be clear at a glance that the rule for this matrix is not based on repetition or a sequence. So what is happening here?

The first three notes you might make about this matrix are:

- The grid is divided into quarters.
- Each section of the grid contains the same-shaped symbol.
- The symbol is shaded half grey and half white.

These points will not lead you to the rule so what else do you notice? Why do none of the three completed sections of the grid look exactly the same? How is the symbol different in each one?

Look at the top half of the grid. In the left section, the white part of the symbol is pointing to the top left-hand corner but in the right section, the white part of the symbol is pointing to the top right-hand corner. Can you think of anything that would cause this change in direction?

Imagine placing a mirror on the dotted line.

What would the mirror image of the symbol look like?

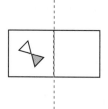

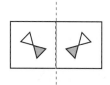

The top right-hand section of the grid is the **reflection** of the top left-hand section.

Now imagine the mirror runs the full length of the grid.

What would the reflection of the bottom left-hand section look like?

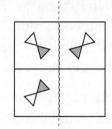

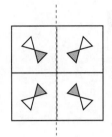

Option **d** has the symbol in the correct position so must be the answer.

Only one mirror line has been shown in the explanation of this example but this matrix actually has four lines of symmetry:

Any of these lines of symmetry may be applied to reflection matrices. In the case of this example, a mirror placed on any of these lines would give you the same grid design, but this will not always be true.

This next example is based on a rule that many children find difficult to see. Others may understand what is happening, but can then find it hard to visualise the answer. This is because it relies on spatial awareness.

REMEMBER!

If you cannot see a reflection on the first mirror line you try, check all other possible directions.

Which shape or pattern completes the larger square? Circle the letter.

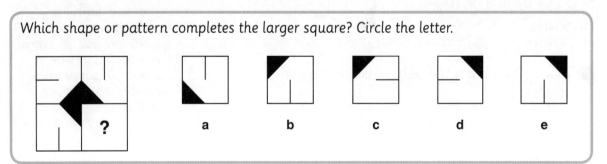

Your first thought could be that this is a reflection question, but a quick assessment to check mirror lines will discount this.

So, first, describe what you can see:

- The grid is divided into quarters.
- Each section contains a short line.
- Each section contains a small, black, right-angled triangle.
- The black triangles appear to form three sides of a square.

As before, break the matrix down into four parts and look at how pairs of sections relate to each other.

Look at the two left-hand sections of the matrix. In the bottom left-hand section the short line is at the bottom of the box and is in a vertical position. In the top left-hand section, the short line is on the left-hand side of the box and is in a horizontal position. What could cause the line to change direction?

Imagine the bottom left-hand section is turned 90 degrees clockwise. What would it look like?

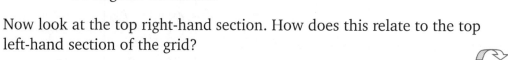

 The top left-hand section of the matrix is the same as the bottom left-hand section rotated 90 degrees clockwise.

Now look at the top right-hand section. How does this relate to the top left-hand section of the grid?

What would the top left-hand section look like if it was also rotated 90 degrees clockwise?

 The top right-hand section of the matrix is the same as the top left-hand section rotated 90 degrees clockwise.

Can you see the rule that has been applied here? This is an example of a **rotation** matrix. You should now be able to predict what the missing section will look like.

Think about what the top right-hand section would look like rotated 90 degrees clockwise.

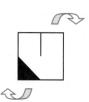

 Option **c** is the only possible answer.

REMEMBER!

If you have difficulty visualising what a shape or symbol will look like when it is rotated clockwise or anticlockwise, try turning the paper round in that direction.

Now it's your turn!

Which shape or pattern completes the larger square? Circle the letter.

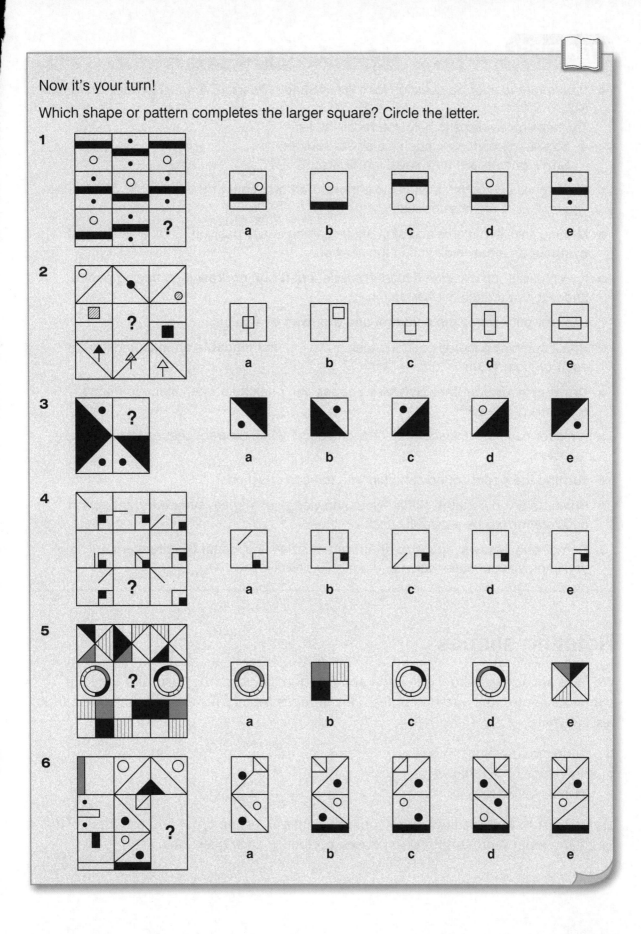

- Remember to check a question for links in **S**hape, **P**osition, **A**ngle, **N**umber, **S**hading, **S**ize.
  Try these mnemonics to help you recall the list:
  - **S**trawberry **p**ancakes **a**nd **n**ice **s**weet **s**auce.
  - **S**uzi's **p**arents **a**re **n**ow **s**peaking **S**panish.

- Sequences and patterns often have **more than one common link** or rule. Make sure you look at all the possibilities.

- Missing links in patterns and sequences can be in any position. Look closely at the **symbols on either side** to find the answer.

- If you have trouble finding a hidden shape, **cut it out**, or **draw it** on tracing paper, and test it over each answer option.

- Look for **patterns in the columns and the rows** of a matrix.

- Break complex patterns or sequences down into **manageable chunks** and look at each section in turn.

- **Drawing arrows or lines between shapes** can often help when trying to match elements of a pattern.

- A **mirror** can help you see what changes occur when different shapes or objects are reflected.

- **Turning the paper round** can help with rotation questions.

- Brush up on your **maths skills** – your knowledge of **angles**, **symmetry**, **reflection** and **rotation** will be especially useful.

- Completing **jigsaws**, **spot-the-difference** puzzles and **visual brainteasers** will help you improve your observation and analysis skills.

Rotating shapes

We have already seen how reflection and rotation can form the basis of a range of non-verbal reasoning question types. This group is based fully around these elements, testing your:

- understanding of symmetry
- knowledge of 3D shapes
- spatial awareness.

Try this test to find out how many rotating shapes question types you can already do. Circle the letter representing your chosen option for each question.

Which shape on the right is the reflection of the shape given on the left?

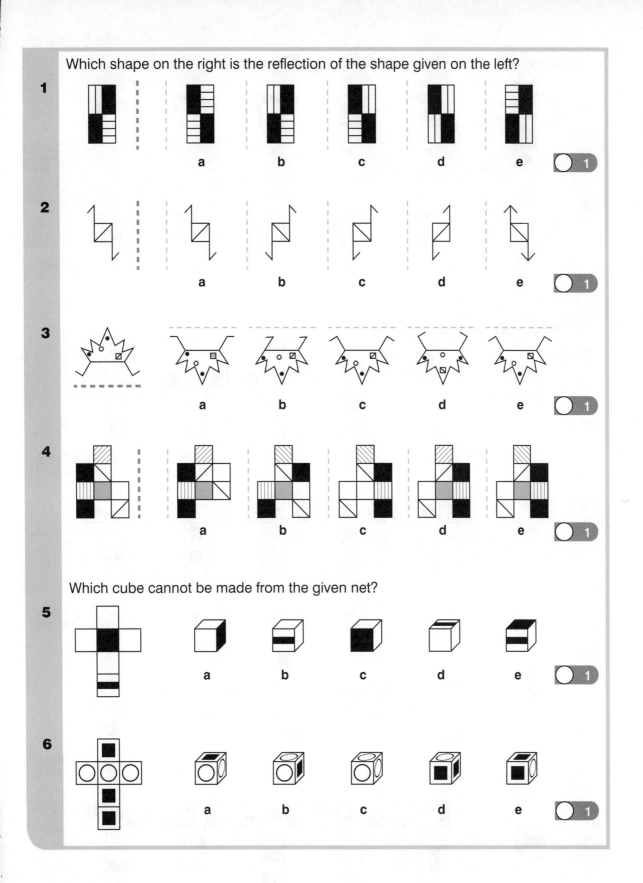

1
    a   b   c   d   e

2
    a   b   c   d   e

3
    a   b   c   d   e

4
    a   b   c   d   e

Which cube cannot be made from the given net?

5
    a   b   c   d   e

6
    a   b   c   d   e

Which cube cannot be made from the given net?

7

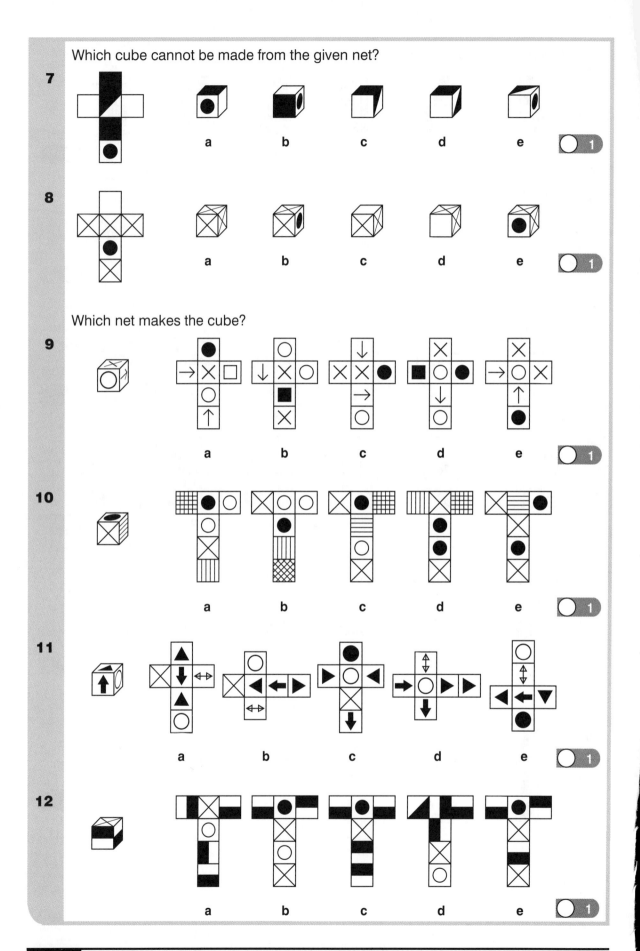

a   b   c   d   e

8

a   b   c   d   e

Which net makes the cube?

9

a   b   c   d   e

10

a   b   c   d   e

11

a   b   c   d   e

12

a   b   c   d   e

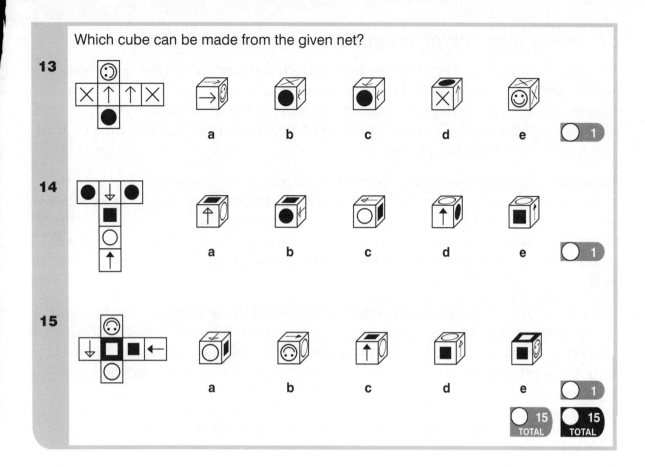

Which cube can be made from the given net?

13

a　　b　　c　　d　　e　　◯ 1

14

a　　b　　c　　d　　e　　◯ 1

15

a　　b　　c　　d　　e　　◯ 1

◯ 15 TOTAL　◯ 15 TOTAL

How did you do?

- Thirteen or more correct? Read the **Top Tips!** and then go on to the next section: Coded shapes and logic.
- Twelve or fewer correct? Work through the question types in this section carefully and then retake the test!

The approach to the questions in this group is slightly different, as you do not need to work out the link between a set of symbols. You will already know from reading the question instructions what rule has been applied to the given shape and the answer options.

There are two main sets of rotating shapes questions:

- Recognise mirror images.
- Link nets to cubes.

Let's start by looking at mirror images.

⑦ Recognise mirror images

This set of questions is often referred to as **reflected shapes**. This type tests your understanding of symmetry and to work out these questions you have to visualise shapes in a new plane. The actual size or number of parts of the given symbol will not change but elements of the mirror image could appear in a different direction or angle and may have changes to shading.

Reflected shapes questions can appear quite straightforward, as you do not have to work out a common link between a set of symbols, imagine a rotated form, or locate a particular section hidden within another symbol. However, subtle differences in the structure or shading of some answer options can catch you out. It is easy to make a careless mistake with this type of question so you need to apply expert observation skills.

You may be able to see the mirror image of a reflected shape straight away but don't worry if you can't. If you remember some key points and follow a logical thought process, you will be able to identify the answer. Let's look at two examples of typical mirror image questions, as well as a range of strategies for practising this question type.

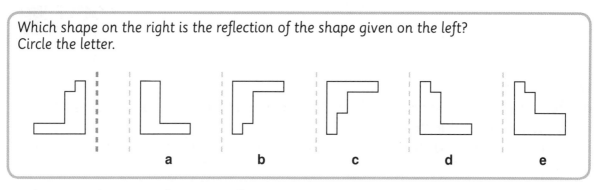

Which shape on the right is the reflection of the shape given on the left? Circle the letter.

a   b   c   d   e

As shown in this example, most reflection questions will place the given shape on one side of a dotted line. This dotted line represents the line of reflection or line of symmetry.

Before you can find the reflection, you must first familiarise yourself with the given symbol.

- How would you describe its basic shape?
- Does it have any noticeable features?
- How many corners or curves does it have?
- Does it have any shaded areas?

You might think that the image in this example reminds you of a set of steps as it has some parts 'cut out' on the left-hand side. You might also notice that it has eight corners and no shading.

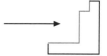

Next, break the shape down into sections and try to imagine a mirror along the line of symmetry. What would the reflection of each part look like? Here are some of the elements you could consider for any given symbol:

- What part of the symbol is closest or furthest away from the mirror?
- Would the horizontal lines change position or direction?
- Would the vertical lines change position or direction?
- Would the diagonal lines change position or direction?
- What would happen to the curved sections?
- How might the direction of any other features (such as arrowheads) change?
- Is there any shading that would look different?

REMEMBER!

Thinking about these types of questions may help you eliminate options straight away.

So for this example you might note that:

The small 'step' is at the top of the shape.

This edge is closest to the mirror.

This edge is furthest from the mirror.

The long 'step' is at the bottom of the shape.

REMEMBER!

Once you are familiar with the given shape, you may find it helpful to quickly sketch what you think the reflection will look like before you look at the options.

Keeping these points in mind, as well as your initial thoughts about the shape, it should now be much easier to compare it with the options to find the right reflection. Make brief notes in a grid if it helps.

	Option a	Option b	Option c	Option d	Option e
Looks like steps?	✗	✓	✓	✓	✓
Small step at the top?	—	✗	✗	✓	✓
Long step at the bottom?	—	—	—	✓	✓

Options **a**, **b** and **c** can be eliminated at this point as they do not meet the criteria. This leaves options **d** and **e**. Compare these two images with the given shape. Which is the mirror image?

Option d   Option e

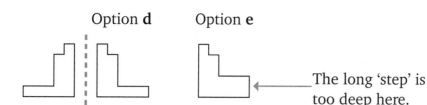

The long 'step' is too deep here.

Following this methodical thought process it is clear that the answer to this example is option **d**.

This line drawing was an example of a simple mirror image question. Now let's look at another example that may appear more complicated but which can be solved by following the same logical, step-by-step technique.

> If you have difficulty imagining a mirror on the line of reflection, try thinking of the given shape as a pattern that has been drawn in ink. If you folded the piece of paper along the dotted line and over the shape, what image would be transferred onto the other side of the paper?

Which shape on the right is the reflection of the shape given on the left? Circle the letter.

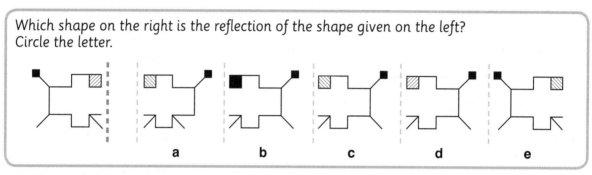

a   b   c   d   e

When symbols are made up of several components it is easy to get confused or to overlook a feature when trying to compare the given shape with the possible reflections. Don't panic! Just break the symbol down into manageable chunks and look at these in turn.

What initial observations can you make about this shape?

The central section of the shape looks like it forms three parts of a cross.

The small black square is furthest away from the line of reflection at the top of the shape.

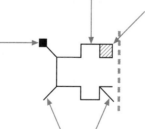

The diagonally-striped square is closest to the line of reflection at the top of the shape.

REMEMBER!

The two short diagonal lines at the bottom of the shape point in opposite directions.

> When looking at the specific features of the given shape, think about their positions in relation to the mirror line. Their reflections will be the same distance from the mirror, just in the opposite direction.

With these elements in mind, look at each of the options quickly. Can any of them be immediately discounted? Yes, option **e** – here the small black square is next to the mirror line.

Now look at the remaining four options more closely and compare them with your notes about the given shape.

Central section looks like three parts of a cross	✓	✓	✓	✓
Diagonally-striped square next to mirror line	✓	✗	✓	✓
Two short diagonal lines at bottom, pointing in opposite directions	✓	—	✓	✓

The reflection is either option **a**, **c** or **d**.

This is where your attention to detail is very important. You now need to look very closely and compare every aspect of each pattern to work out how they differ.

Option a

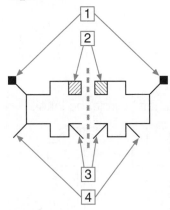

1 Small black square in correct position. ✓

2 Striped shading in correct direction. ✓

3 Short diagonal line in correct position and direction. ✓

4 Second diagonal line in correct position. ✗

Option **a** cannot be the answer.

Option c

1 Small black square in correct position. ✓

2 Striped shading in correct direction. ✓

3 Short diagonal line in correct position and direction. ✓

4 Second diagonal line in correct position and direction. ✓

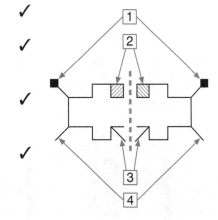

Option **c** appears to have all of the elements in the correct positions but check option **d** quickly just to be sure!

Option d

1 Small black square in correct position. ✓

2 Striped shading in correct direction. ✗

There is no need to continue the comparison as the diagonally-striped shading has not been reflected. Option **d** cannot be the answer.

This confirms that option **c** shows the reflection of this complex shape.

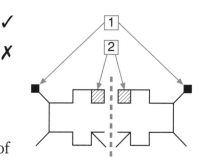

REMEMBER!

If you want to see what happens to different types of shapes when they are reflected, draw a range of shapes and place a mirror next to them. Or draw over the shapes with tracing paper and, without rotating it, flip the tracing paper over horizontally and see what happens to each shape. The more familiar you are with how shapes do or don't change when reflected, the easier these questions will become.

REMEMBER!

A mirror line might not always be to the right of the given shape. It may be on the left or above or below the original symbol, so pay close attention to the direction in which the shape is being reflected. Wherever the mirror line is, you can still use the techniques shown here to find the reflection.

Now it's your turn!

Which shape on the right is the reflection of the shape given on the left? Circle the letter.

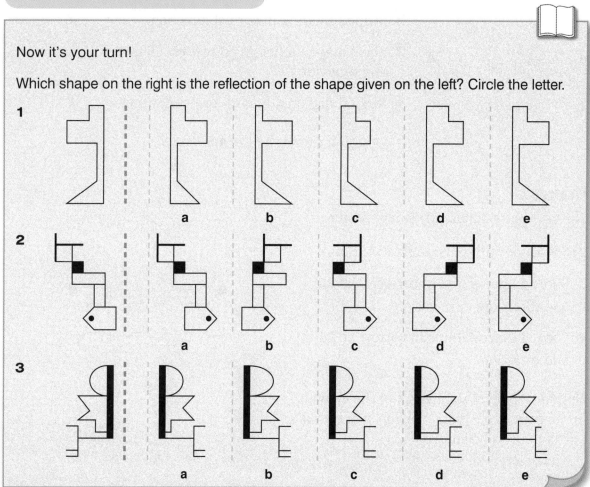

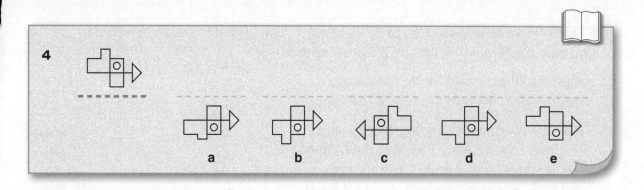

4

a   b   c   d   e

⑧ *Link nets to cubes*

The questions in this group are called **nets** and they test your spatial awareness. Many people struggle with this type of question as you have to think in three-dimensional terms. You need to be able to relate a two-dimensional outline, or net, to a three-dimensional shape and this can be hard to visualise.

There are 11 different ways that a cube can be cut to make a net. However, it is unlikely that you will need to be familiar with all of these versions for non-verbal reasoning as these questions often only involve three styles of net: the vertical cross, the horizontal cross and the T-shape.

The vertical cross   **The horizontal cross**   **The T-shape**

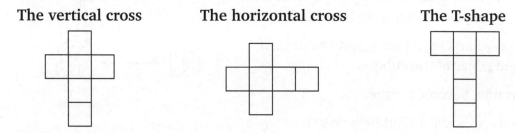

Whatever style of net a question is based on, there are some basic rules that can help you visualise any net as a solid cube. Let's explore these rules in relation to the vertical cross.

a   Try to think of a cube as having four sides, a top and a bottom. Each of these is represented by one of the six **faces** that form the net.
These faces are connected by five **joints**. When the net is folded, these joints will become five out of the 12 **edges** of the cube.

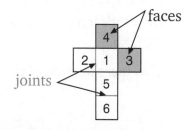

This leaves seven edges, which are created as the cube is formed. These edges are made by folding the net along the joints and joining the faces together. You can think of it as drawing two pieces of material together and sewing a **seam**.

Some of these seams are easier to visualise than others, so we'll start with the more straightforward ones!

REMEMBER!

Depending on how you fold a net, any face can be viewed as the top, side or bottom of the cube.

STEP 1. First, let's look at faces 4, 2, 1 and 3. The blue lines show which pairs of adjacent borders will form the first two seams.

Imagine folding face 4 along the dotted joint to make this face the top of the cube.

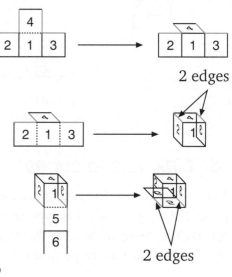

2 edges

STEP 2. Now imagine folding faces 2 and 3 along the dotted joints. Face 4 is now joined together with faces 2 and 3, forming two seams or edges of the cube. Faces 1, 2 and 3 have become three sides of the cube.

STEP 3. This leaves faces 5 and 6. First, think about folding face 5 along the dotted joint, so it sits underneath the shape. Again, the blue lines show which adjacent borders will meet up.

Face 5 is now joined to faces 2 and 3, forming two more edges, and it has become the bottom of the cube.

2 edges

STEP 4. The cube now has a top, a bottom and three sides. Imagine folding face 6 along the dotted joint so that the three pairs of opposite blue borders meet.

3 edges

Face 6 is now joined with face 4 and has formed the last three edges of the cube.

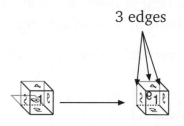

The net has now become a cube.

This stepped approach should help you to see how a 2D net can be folded to create a 3D cube. It shows which pairs of **adjacent face borders join together** to make the missing seven edges of the cube.

REMEMBER!

Faces that are connected by joints in a net will always be next to each other in a cube.

b Now let's look at the next rule that can help you to visualise how a net can become a 3D shape.

Two faces in each of these nets have been shaded.

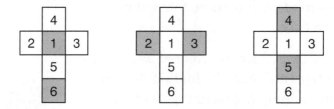

What do you notice about the positions of these pairs of faces in the cubes?

Alternate faces in a net end up opposite each other when folded into a cube so, using the numbering system shown for the vertical cross:

- Face 1 will always be opposite face 6.
- Face 2 will always be opposite face 3.
- Face 4 will always be opposite face 5.

c There is one more rule you need to think about when solving net questions and it can be the trickiest to visualise as it involves your understanding of **rotation**.

When imagining how a net will fold up to make a cube, you need to think about whether the direction or orientation of any symbols will change as each face is folded along the joints.

To help, let's put a symbol onto the net, starting with face 6. Here is the net again at Step 3 in **a** above.

What do you think will happen to the arrow as face 6 is folded to form the back of the cube? Look at Steps 3 and 4 again. What do you notice?

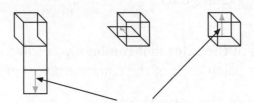

As face 6 has been folded to meet face 4, the direction of the arrow has changed. In the completed cube the arrow appears to be reversed, now pointing up instead of down.

For the next example it is helpful to compare a section of the vertical cross with a section of the T-shaped net.

Here are faces 4, 2 and 1 of the vertical cross as seen at Step 2 in **a** above.

Do you think the orientation of the arrow will change as face 2 is folded to meet face 4?

No, the direction of the horizontal arrow has not changed as face 2 has been folded.

Now let's look at what happens when face 2 is folded in the T-shape.

As in the vertical cross, faces 2, 4 and 1 are connected, but here it is the adjacent borders of face 2 and face 1 that meet.

	2	4	3
		1	
		5	
		6	

Now imagine that face 4 is folded along the dotted joint, forming the top of the cube.

Let's also place a horizontal arrow on face 2 as before.

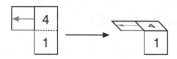

After this move the arrow is still in a horizontal position.

Now visualise folding face 2 along the dotted joint, so that it meets face 1 and forms a seam, or an edge of the cube.

What has happened to the orientation of the arrow?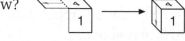

With the second fold, the direction of the arrow appears to have changed. The horizontal arrow has become vertical.

These two stepped examples show that:
- **a symbol on the net face that forms the back of the cube when folded may become reversed**
- **a symbol on a face that is folded more than once may change its orientation.**

REMEMBER!

One of the best ways to visualise how cubes are made from nets is to actually draw and cut out some nets yourself. Then, number the faces and see what happens as you fold them together along the joints to create the cube. To help you get started, you can find a range of nets for cubes on our web site. Just follow the Free Resources link.

Now that we have looked at the rules that can help you solve net questions, let's look at three worked examples using each of the common styles of net.

The first example is based on the vertical cross.

Which cube cannot be made from the given net? Circle the letter.

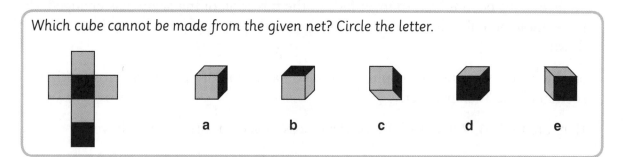

This version of a net question shows a vertical cross and is asking you to find the one cube that **cannot be made** from this net.

You may be able to see the answer straight away, but if not, work through the three rules and think about the answer options at each stage:

REMEMBER!

These three versions of net questions use very similar wording so read the instructions carefully to make sure you know what you are being asked to do.

1 **Work out which adjacent borders will meet to form the seams, or edges, of the 3D cube.**

This may not help you to eliminate any options for this example as there are so many faces that have light-grey shading.

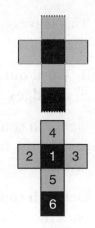

2 **Identify which faces will be opposite each other when the cube is formed.**

When comparing the pairs of opposites with the options, it should be clear that option **d** may be the answer as this shows two adjacent black faces.

Faces 1 and 6 are the only black faces in the net and these would be opposite, not next to each other, when the cube was formed.

3 **Look out for any symbols that could be rotated as the faces are folded.**

There are no symbols in this net and no shading that could rotate, so this rule does not apply to this example.

Option **d** must therefore be the answer – it cannot be made from the given net as the faces are not shown in the correct positions.

This next example uses the horizontal cross.

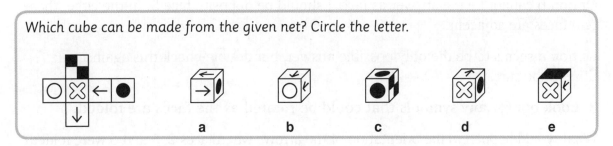

Which cube can be made from the given net? Circle the letter.

a   b   c   d   e

First, make sure you understand what the question is asking. Here you need to find one cube that **can be made** from the net.

Net questions may seem more confusing when they involve symbols. However, there is a quick trick you can try to eliminate some options before you think about the three rules.

Scan each answer option, comparing the symbols or shading that the cubes contain with those in the net. If any cubes have a type of symbol or shading not present in the net, you know that these options cannot be made and can therefore be eliminated.

A quick look at the answer options and the net in this example should show you that options **c** and **e** can be eliminated immediately:

- Option **c** shows two black circles; the net only has one black circle.
- Option **e** shows a top face shaded black; the net does not have a black face.

This leaves options **a**, **b** and **d** which you can now think about in relation to the three rules.

1 Work out which adjacent opposite borders will meet to form the seams, or edges, of the 3D cube.

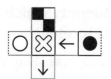

Option **a** could be the answer as the black circle is connected by a joint to the horizontal arrow and it would be joined to the vertical arrow when the adjacent borders met.

Option **b** could be the answer as the white circle would be joined with the vertical arrow when their adjacent borders met.

Option **d** cannot be the answer. The black circle would not be joined to the cross so this can be eliminated.

2 Identify which faces will be opposite each other when the cube is formed.

	3		
4	1	5	6
	2		

Option **a** could be the answer as:

- you cannot see what is opposite face 6
- you cannot see what is opposite face 5
- you cannot see what is opposite face 2.

Option **b** cannot be the answer as face 4 should be opposite face 5. In the cube, these two faces are adjacent.

Option **a** seems to be the only possible answer, but double-check this against rule three to be sure.

3 Look out for any symbols that could be rotated as the faces are folded.

What would happen to the orientation of the arrows when faces 2, 5 and 6 were folded?

Imagine folding the cube around face 5, making this the top of the cube.

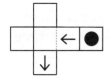

Start by folding the dotted joint between face 1 and face 5.

Next, fold face 2 along the dotted joint so it forms a seam with face 5. Notice the change in orientation of the arrow.

Now fold face 6 so it forms a seam with face 2.

Does this look like option **a**?

Yes.

- The arrow on face 5 is still facing away from the circle on face 6.
- The arrow on face 2 is now horizontal and pointing towards face 6.

Option **a** is the correct answer.

The final example is based on the T-shape net and it follows a different format to the other two versions. In this style of net question, you are given a cube and you have to work out which net has been used to create it. You may find this format confusing at first but you can still apply the same rules and step-by-step techniques to work out the answer.

REMEMBER!

Turning the paper round can often help you imagine what would happen to a face if it were folded along a joint.

Which net makes the cube? Circle the letter.

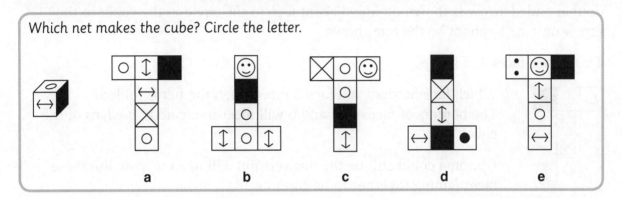

First, scan the nets and check whether any of the options can be eliminated straight away. As you can only see the top and two sides of the cube you do not know what symbols or shading will be on the rest of the faces. You can therefore only eliminate a net at this stage if it does not contain all three of the given cube faces.

Can any nets be eliminated? Yes, option **d**. It does not have a white circle so cannot be the answer.

This leaves options **a**, **b**, **c** and **e** to consider in relation to the three rules.

It might be easier to look at option **c** first as this only contains one double-ended arrow, whereas the other three options have two double-ended arrows.

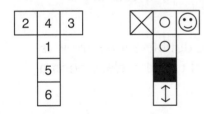

Concentrate on the faces that have the same symbols as shown in the cube. So for option **c** these are faces 4, 1, 5 and 6.

Faces 4 and 1 both show a circle. Think about which one of these could be showing on the top of the cube.

You know that face 1 and face 6 will be opposite each other when the cube is folded. The cube shows the circle and the double-ended arrow on adjacent faces, so face 1 cannot be the top of the cube.

Now look at the second circle. You know that face 4 and face 5 will be opposite each other when the cube is folded. The cube shows the circle and the black shaded side on adjacent faces, so face 4 cannot be the top of the cube.

Option **c** can be discounted. Work through the remaining options from left to right to make sure you look at each one in the same way.

Here is option **a**.

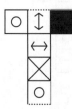

Faces 2 and 3 will be opposite when the net is folded but the cube shows the circle and black shaded side on adjacent faces. The circle on face 2 therefore cannot be on the top of the cube.

Now look at face 6. Faces 1 and 6 will also be opposite when the cube is formed. The double-ended arrow is shown on an adjacent face to the circle in the cube, so the arrow on face 1 cannot be the one shown.

This leaves faces 4, 3 and 6.

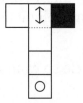

Which face borders will face 6 meet when the net is folded? The borders of faces 4, 3 and 6 will meet to create two edges of the cube.

Option **a** could still be the answer. You will need to visualise these faces joining together to be sure.

Imagine folding the cube around face 1, making this the front of the cube.

Start by folding the dotted joint between face 4 and face 1 so face 4 forms the top of the cube.

Next, fold face 5 along the dotted joint so it forms the bottom of the cube.

Now fold face 6 so it forms a seam with face 4.

Look at the direction of the arrow in relation to the circle on face 6.

Is it the same orientation as in the given cube? No, here the double-ended arrow is pointing towards the circle. In the cube, the arrow is parallel to the circle. Option **a** can be eliminated.

Let's move on to option **b**.

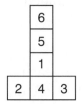 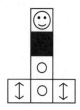

This net may look a bit confusing initially but it is still the T-shape; it has just been turned upside down. You can still examine it in the same way.

Look at the circle on face 4. You know that face 4 and face 5 will be opposite each other when the net is folded. In the cube, the circle is shown on an adjacent face to the black shaded square. Face 4 therefore cannot be the top of the cube.

This means you need to look at faces 2, 3, 1 and 5.

Think about how the borders of these faces will meet up to create the edges of the cube.

Fold face 4 along the dotted joint so it becomes the bottom of the cube.

Now fold faces 2 and 3 upwards along the dotted joints.

What do you notice about the double-ended arrows? They have both changed direction and are now pointing towards the circle.

Option **b** can also be discounted at this point as the double-ended arrow should be parallel to the circle.

This leaves option **e** which, by this process of elimination, must be the answer. Remember though, even if you think you have found the correct answer, it is always best to double-check.

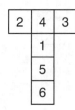 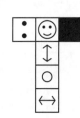

So, look at faces 3, 1, 5 and 6. How will the borders of these faces join to form edges of the cube? Follow the same step-by-step process as for the previous options.

Look at face 6. It has the same symbol as the front face of the given cube. So, to make the folding stages easier to visualise, imagine folding the net around face 6, keeping it as the front face.

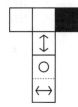

Fold face 5 along the dotted joint, making it the top of the cube.

Then fold face 1 along the dotted joint to form the back of the cube.

Next, fold face 4 along the dotted joint, making this face the bottom of the cube.

Can you see that this is the same as the given cube? If not, imagine folding face 3 upwards along the dotted joint to meet face 5.

The given cube shows faces 6, 5 and 3 of option **e**. Option **e** is the correct answer.

REMEMBER!

When solving a net question, think of EOR:
Edges
Opposites
Rotation

Questions that require spatial awareness, such as nets of cubes, are often one of the most difficult non-verbal reasoning question types for children to grasp. If your child finds it hard to visualise a 2D diagram as a 3D object, spend some time together looking at how nets work. Draw, cut out and fold different nets to see how they create 3D shapes; unfold a range of cardboard packaging, such as cereal boxes, and see how they are put together etc. If you're a bit rusty on drawing nets, follow the Free Resources link on our web site to download some sample nets of cubes.

Now it's your turn!

Which cube cannot be made from the given net? Circle the letter.

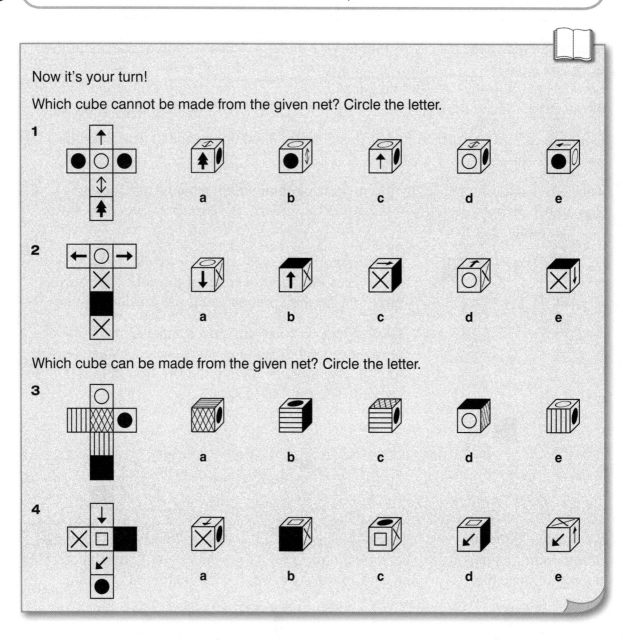

Which cube can be made from the given net? Circle the letter.

Which net makes the cube? Circle the letter.

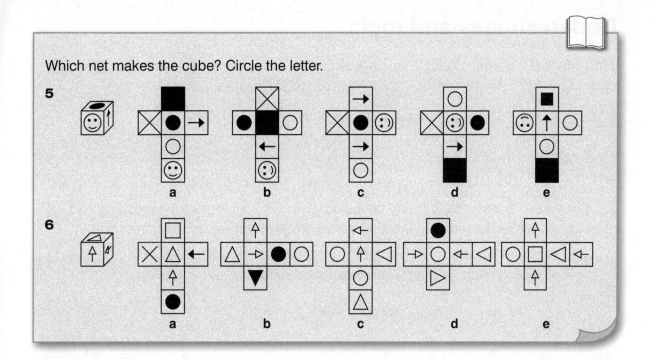

TOP TIPS!

- **Break a shape down** into sections and think about what the reflection of each part would look like.

- **Sketching** your predicted reflection can help you identify the answer quickly.

- Reflections will be the **same distance from the mirror line** as the original shape, just in the opposite direction.

- The **line of reflection can be placed anywhere** near a shape; check the direction in which shapes are being reflected.

- **Differences in structure and shading are often subtle**. Check the detail of each option carefully to find the right answer.

- Draw, cut out and **make your own 3D shapes from nets.** This is the best way to understand how a 2D plan relates to a 3D object.

- **Looking for symbols that do not appear** in a net or on a cube can be a quick way of eliminating answer options.

- **Turning the paper round** can help when you need to visualise folding a net into a cube.

- When solving nets, remember: **EOR**! **E**dges, **O**pposites, **R**otation. Try one of these mnemonics or make up your own:
  - **E**lves **O**n **R**eindeer!
  - **E**ject **O**r **R**ewind?
  - **E**levate **O**r **R**aze?

- Try **3D shape-building puzzles** and **tiling games** (for example, Katamino). They will help you to improve your spatial awareness.

Coded shapes and logic

This group of questions tests your understanding of shape but you also need to apply your logic skills. To solve these questions you need the ability to:

- think systematically and make deductions about a set of symbols
- find and apply a given rule
- identify common features
- see shapes within shapes.

Try this test to find out how many coded shapes and logic question types you can already do. Circle the letter representing your chosen option for each question.

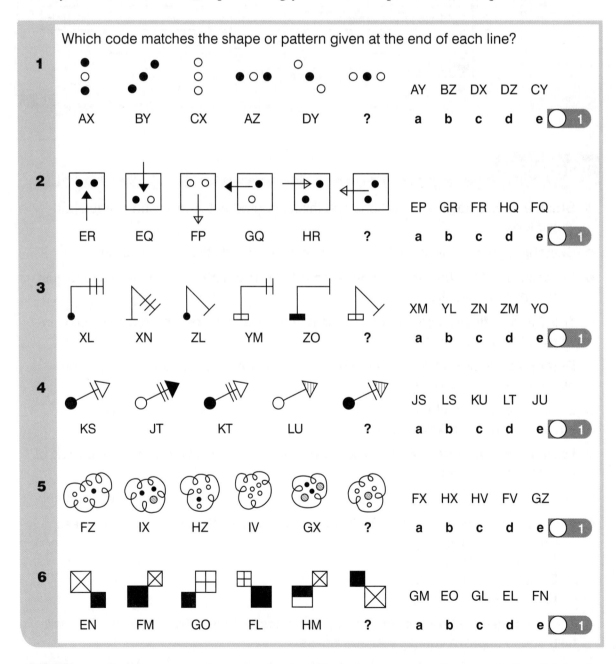

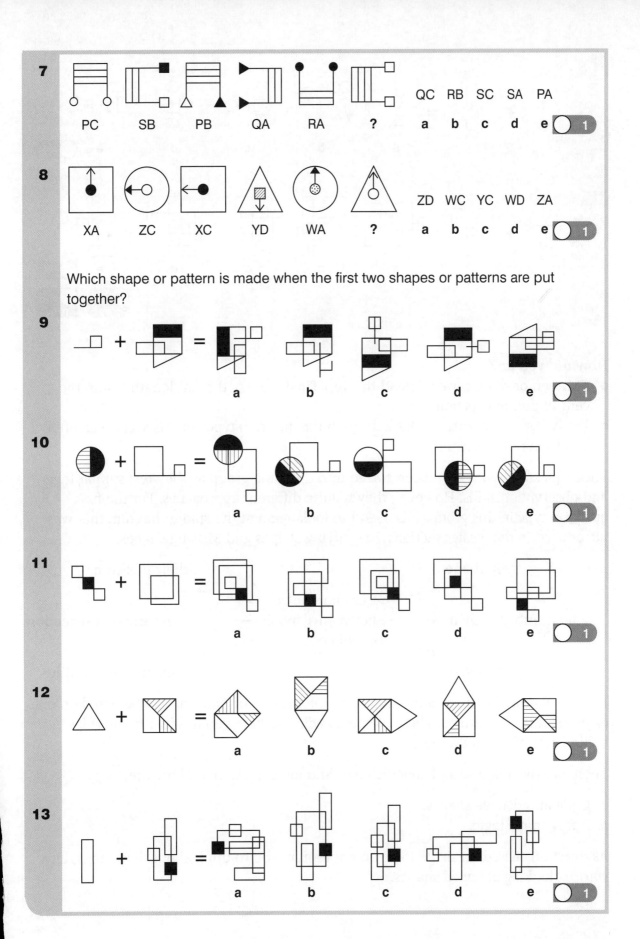

7

PC   SB   PB   QA   RA   ?

QC   RB   SC   SA   PA
a   b   c   d   e   ○ 1

8

XA   ZC   XC   YD   WA   ?

ZD   WC   YC   WD   ZA
a   b   c   d   e   ○ 1

Which shape or pattern is made when the first two shapes or patterns are put together?

9

a   b   c   d   e   ○ 1

10

a   b   c   d   e   ○ 1

11

a   b   c   d   e   ○ 1

12

a   b   c   d   e   ○ 1

13

a   b   c   d   e   ○ 1

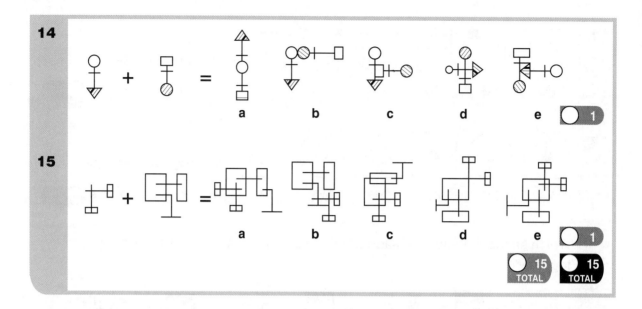

14 ... a b c d e ○ 1

15 ... a b c d e ○ 1

○ 15 TOTAL ○ 15 TOTAL

How did you do?

- Thirteen or more correct? Read the **Top Tips!** and try the full-length test in the central pull-out section.
- Twelve or fewer correct? Work through the question types in this section carefully and then retake the test!

These question types have been sorted into the same group as they test similar logic and observation skills. However, they require different approaches. For the first question type in this group, it is useful to look again at the spider diagram that was introduced in the earlier sections, Identifying shapes and Missing shapes:

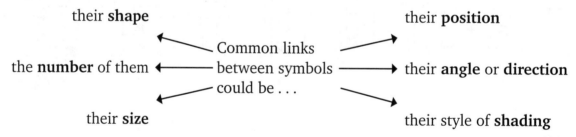

their **shape**   their **position**

the **number** of them ← Common links between symbols could be ... → their **angle** or **direction**

their **size**   their style of **shading**

You know now that links between a series of symbols or patterns can be based on one or more of these features. These elements will also help you to identify the rules behind sets of coded symbols.

There are two main sets of coded shapes and logic questions. These are:

- Code and decode shapes.
- Apply shape logic.

As questions based on shape logic do not require you to think about these links, let's start by looking at coded shapes.

⑨ Code and decode shapes

These questions are often referred to as **codes** or **coded sequences**. You may be familiar with this type of question from verbal reasoning papers. In both verbal and non-verbal reasoning, questions involving codes test your logic and deduction skills as well as your ability to work out and follow sequences and patterns. The difference with non-verbal reasoning codes is that you have to understand how visual features relate to letter codes, rather than how words relate to them.

Usually a question will present a series of patterns or symbols in a line, with each symbol except one having a unique code that is made up of two letters. You must then use your analysis skills to work out the rule behind the code and apply it correctly to find the missing code for the unlabelled symbol.

Let's look at a straightforward example.

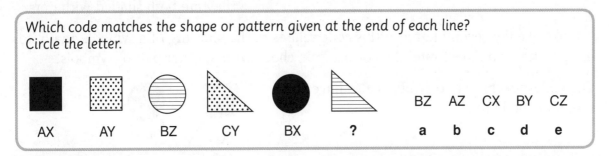

All codes stand for, or represent, something else. In the case of non-verbal reasoning, each letter of a code will represent a different feature or element of the given series of symbols. The first letter in each code will always stand for the same feature throughout the series. Similarly, the next letter of each code will stand for a second element throughout the whole series.

You need to find a connection between two or more symbols that share part of the code. The most effective way to do this is to approach the question systematically.

Start by looking at each coded symbol.

Are there any symbols that share their first code letter? Yes.

These two symbols must therefore have a common feature.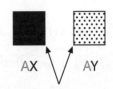

These are both squares.

It looks like the first letter of this code relates to the **shape** of a symbol. To be sure that you have found the correct link for the first letter, check if any more symbols share the same first code letter.

The codes for these two symbols also start with the same letter.

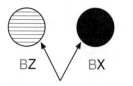

They are both circles.

This confirms that the first letter of the code reflects the shape of a symbol.

Now think about the second code letters.

Are there any symbols that share their second letter? Yes.

What do these symbols have in common?

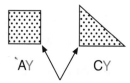

They are both shaded with dots.

It looks like the second letter of this code relates to the **shading** of a symbol. Again, to be sure that you have found the correct link, check with another pair of symbols.

The codes for these two symbols also have the same second letter.

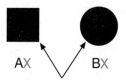

They are both shaded black.

This confirms that the second letter of the code reflects the shading of a symbol.

Now that you have worked out the rules behind the code, you can find the missing code for the unlabelled symbol.

Think about what the symbol is: a right-angled triangle with horizontally-striped shading.

Now look for the symbols that share the same shape and shading.

The code for the unlabelled symbol must be CZ, option **e**.

CY   BZ

☀ REMEMBER!

If you cannot find the link immediately, try describing what you can see as this can help you focus on common elements.

☀ REMEMBER!

Sometimes a code question will be presented in a different format (in a grid for example) or the code will have been formed using more than two digits and a combination of letters and numbers. If you are given a set of questions in a different format, don't panic! You can still use the same logical thought processes to find the missing code.

☀ REMEMBER!

As for many question types, make sure you work from left to right to ensure you don't overlook any elements.

Now it's your turn!

Which code matches the shape or pattern given at the end of each line? Circle the letter.

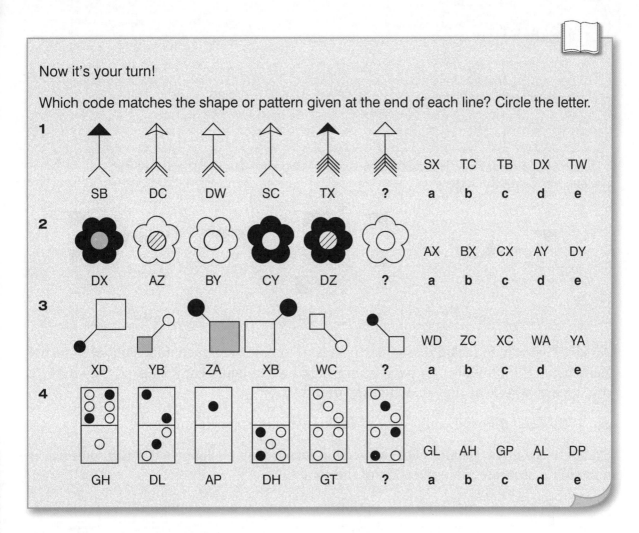

1

						SX	TC	TB	DX	TW
SB	DC	DW	SC	TX	?	a	b	c	d	e

2

						AX	BX	CX	AY	DY
DX	AZ	BY	CY	DZ	?	a	b	c	d	e

3

						WD	ZC	XC	WA	YA
XD	YB	ZA	XB	WC	?	a	b	c	d	e

4

						GL	AH	GP	AL	DP
GH	DL	AP	DH	GT	?	a	b	c	d	e

⑩ Apply shape logic

The questions in this set are often called **combined shapes**. Usually a question in this group will show you two shapes and ask you to select the shape or pattern that is made when they are combined. In a similar way to hidden shapes questions, you therefore need to use your powers of observation and analysis to spot individual shapes within given patterns.

This question type may seem very straightforward, as questions do not rely on you finding common links between a group of symbols. Although the size or style of shading of the individual shapes will not change when they are combined, they may be rotated and appear at a different angle within the combined pattern. They may also overlap each other, which can make the individual shapes difficult to identify. As with all non-verbal reasoning questions, make sure you look at all aspects carefully to avoid making careless mistakes.

Some combined shapes questions will be easier to work out than others. Don't worry if you cannot see an answer straight away. If you approach these questions methodically, you will be able to find the answer. Let's look at an example that may appear quite difficult at first glance.

✔ **PARENT TIP**

If your child has difficulty identifying the correct option, encourage them to draw over the given shapes on a piece of tracing paper (greaseproof paper works well). They can then place these images over the combined shapes to locate the two individual symbols. Make sure they do not flip the tracing paper over – the symbols in the correct option will not be reflected.

Which shape or pattern is made when the first two shapes or patterns are put together? Circle the letter.

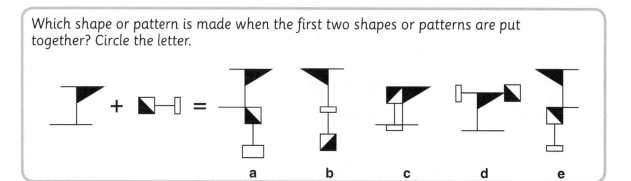

a   b   c   d   e

An effective way to tackle these questions is to look for each separate symbol in turn. Remember, the symbols may have been rotated when being combined, so they may not appear exactly as they do when separated.

So, in this example you could start by looking at the first symbol.

Compare the given symbol with the version included in each option. Which options contain an accurate representation of the symbol?

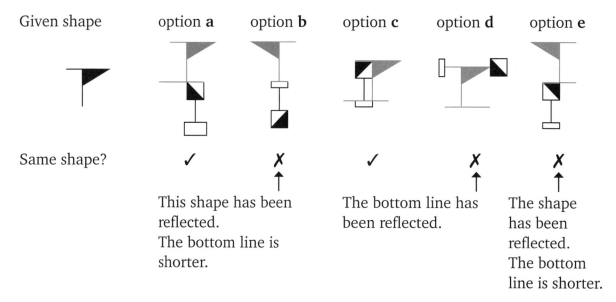

Given shape	option **a**	option **b**	option **c**	option **d**	option **e**

Same shape?	✓	✗ ↑	✓	✗ ↑	✗ ↑
		This shape has been reflected. The bottom line is shorter.		The bottom line has been reflected.	The shape has been reflected. The bottom line is shorter.

Examining the first symbol in each of the options has shown that options **b**, **d** and **e** cannot be the correct answer. These can therefore be eliminated.

Now compare the versions of the second symbol in options **a** and **c**. Which one shows an exact copy?

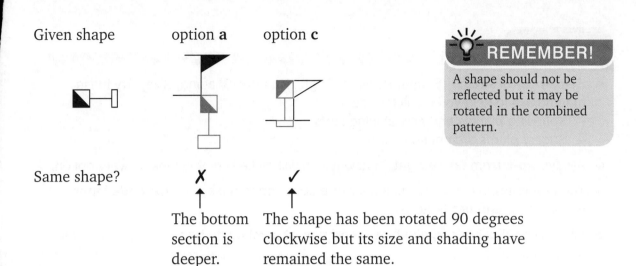

Given shape option **a** option **c**

REMEMBER!

A shape should not be reflected but it may be rotated in the combined pattern.

Same shape?

The bottom section is deeper.

The shape has been rotated 90 degrees clockwise but its size and shading have remained the same.

Option **c** must therefore be the correct answer.

Now it's your turn!

Which shape or pattern is made when the first two shapes or patterns are put together? Circle the letter.

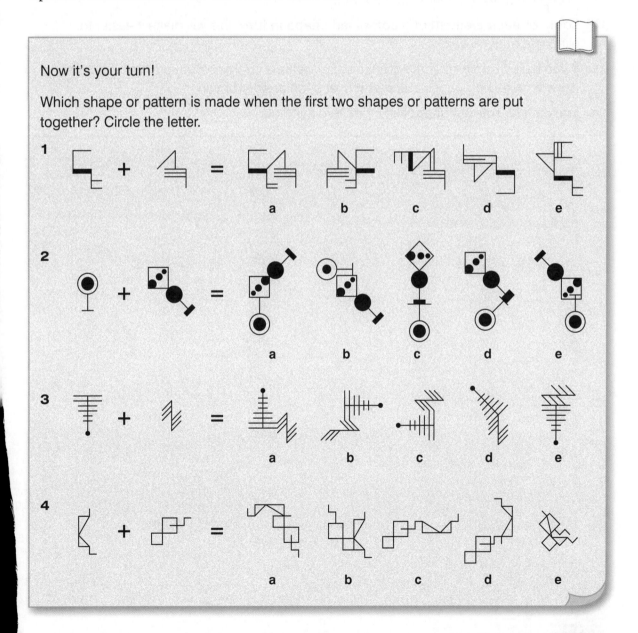

- Remember **SPANSS**! (**S**hape, **P**osition, **A**ngle, **N**umber, **S**hading, **S**ize). Try these mnemonics to help you recall the list:
  - **S**parkling **p**lanets **a**nd **n**ew **s**hining **s**tars.
  - **S**ugary **p**lums **a**re **n**ot **s**o **s**harp!

- Always **work from left to right**. That way you will make sure you look at every option.

- The **first letter** in a code will stand for **one common feature**, the **next code letter** will stand for **another feature**.

- Always **check a code against a second pair of symbols** to be sure you have found the correct rules.

- **Differences in structure and shading are often subtle.** Check the detail of each option carefully to find the right answer.

- **Look for each element of a combined shape in turn**; this will make it easier to eliminate options quickly.

- If you have trouble finding a given symbol within a combined pattern, **cut it out**, or **draw it** on tracing paper, and **test it** over each answer option.

- Look out for **rotated shapes** in combined symbols.

C: How do you prepare for the exam?

① What next?

Now that you have successfully worked through this book, use the detachable full-length paper to check what you have learnt. If you attempted the test paper before reading this book, have another go and compare your scores. You can download another free copy from our web site (www.bond11plus.co.uk) via the Free Resources link. For more practice on all the key non-verbal reasoning question types, work through the range of books and test papers in the Bond 11+ non-verbal reasoning range.

Mark your answers with an adult. Look carefully at any questions you get wrong or find difficult. Read back through the step-by-step techniques and worked examples given in this book to make sure you fully understand each type. This will help you remember how to tackle the trickier questions when you are in the exam.

② Build confidence with practice

To give yourself the best chance, start practising well before the exam date. If you begin a regular weekly routine about a year before the exam (when you enter Year 5) you will have plenty of time to practise a wide range of question types. The full range of Bond non-verbal reasoning papers will give you plenty of opportunities to practise your skills, improve your understanding and build your confidence.

Here are some useful tips to remember before you start your practice routine:

Checklist

- ✔ Check what subjects the exam covers and what format the papers will follow.
- ✔ Note down the date, time and place of the exam.
- ✔ Plan something fun to do after the exam – this will give you and your family a reward to look forward to.
- ✔ Some children find it helpful to create a timeline showing how long they have to practise before the exam day.

✔ PARENT TIP

For more advice on practice routines and useful techniques, read The Parents' Guide to the 11+.

③ Time yourself

You may find it helpful to work through your first few *Bond Assessment Papers in Non-verbal Reasoning* slowly, so you can get used to the types of questions and format of the papers. Once you are familiar with many of the different question types and the strategies needed to solve them it is important that you start timing yourself. The final exam will be timed (you may only have 30 minutes to complete it) so if you set yourself a similar timeframe for practice papers you will be able to pace yourself.

It is likely that, for the first few times you set a time limit, the time will run out before you finish a paper. Don't worry. When the time is up just put a mark against the last question you answered in time, then work through to the end of the paper as quickly as you can. This will show you how far away you were from the end of the paper when the time was up.

When you have finished, think about where you spent the most time. Which questions took the longest to answer? Why? Was it because you weren't sure how to solve them or did the questions just require a more detailed process to find the answer? When you have identified these types, read back through the relevant strategies and tips in this book and spend time just practising these question types. Doing this will improve your techniques for solving them, which will help to reduce the amount of time you need to find the answers. You should then be able to spread your time more evenly across a paper and complete it in the set timeframe.

(4) Revise strategies and techniques

There are lots of tips in this book that will help you to improve your logic and reasoning skills, as well as specific strategies showing you how to solve a wide range of key question types. Check back through the Top Tips! as well as the Remember! Boxes given throughout each section.

You may not have had much experience of exams before you take the 11+, so it can be helpful to spend some time thinking about good techniques to use in the exam. The following section gives you some essential advice on how to prepare for the day itself.

(5) The exam day itself

Here are some useful tips to remember for the night before and during the exam:

The night before

Checklist

- ✓ Avoid doing last-minute practice as it can make you nervous.
- ✓ Relax! Try reading a book, having a bath, playing a game or listening to music.
- ✓ Have an early night so you can have a good night's sleep.

On the day

Checklist

- ✓ Make sure you get up in plenty of time to have a good energising breakfast.
- ✓ Arrive in plenty of time so you're not rushing in just before the exam starts.
- ✓ Take one or two pencils, a pencil sharpener and an eraser. Remember to keep any necessary medication with you (such as an inhaler). Your parents may need to tell the exam supervisor if you have a medical condition. Some tissues might also be useful.
- ✓ Find out where the toilets are (and go if you can) before the test begins.

In the exam room

✓ **Find the clock.** Knowing where the clock is will enable you to make some quick time checks during the test.

✓ **Check the paper.** Spend a minute flicking through the paper before you start so you know how many questions there are. This will ensure you don't forget to turn over the last page and answer the final set of questions.

✓ **Try to relax!** You have done lots of practice papers so the paper format should be familiar and if you have practised a wide range of question types there should be few surprises.

✓ **Concentrate.** Settle down and stay focused. Try to ignore any distractions that may occur during the exam.

✓ **Read each question.** Read slowly and carefully to make sure you know what a question is asking.

✓ **Write answers carefully.** If the paper is a multiple-choice format, make sure you mark each answer box carefully in the separate answer booklet. You could lose marks if your answers are not clearly shaded in the right box. If the paper is a standard format, write your answers neatly in the spaces provided and cross through any mistakes clearly.

✓ **Don't panic!** If you can't do a question, make a mark next to it and move on. You can come back to it later when you have answered the rest of the questions.

✓ **Avoid leaving a blank.** Remember, a logical guess can often be right so always have a go.

✓ **Allow time for checking.** Try to finish a few minutes before the end of the exam so you can check your answers.

✓ **Do your best.** You cannot expect more of yourself than that!

GOOD LUCK!

Answers

Identifying shapes

Test (p. 5)

1	d	**9**	c
2	a	**10**	b
3	e	**11**	b
4	c	**12**	c
5	a	**13**	b
6	c	**14**	d
7	d	**15**	e
8	c		

(1) Recognise shapes that are similar and different

Practice box (p. 13)

1	b	**4**	d
2	d	**5**	b
3	a	**6**	e

(2) Identify shapes and patterns

Practice box (p. 16)

1	a	**3**	c
2	e	**4**	b

(3) Pair up shapes

Worked example (p. 21)

d

Practice box (p. 25)

1	e	**4**	c
2	c	**5**	e
3	b	**6**	d

Missing shapes

Test (p. 26)

1	e	**9**	c
2	d	**10**	b
3	a	**11**	d
4	c	**12**	d
5	e	**13**	c
6	e	**14**	d
7	e	**15**	b
8	c		

(4) Find shapes that complete a sequence

Practice box (p. 39)

1 b	**5** d
2 e	**6** d
3 b	**7** b
4 a	

(5) Find a given part within a shape

Practice box (p. 43)

1 a	**3** a
2 e	**4** d

(6) Find a missing shape from a pattern

Practice box (p. 51)

1 d	**4** d
2 a	**5** c
3 c	**6** b

Rotating shapes

Test (p. 53)

1 c	**9** b
2 b	**10** c
3 e	**11** b
4 e	**12** e
5 e	**13** e
6 c	**14** d
7 e	**15** e
8 a	

(7) Recognise mirror images

Practice box (p. 60)

1 e	**3** c
2 d	**4** d

(8) Link nets to cubes

Practice box (p. 70)

1 c	**4** d
2 e	**5** b
3 b	**6** e

Coded shapes and logic

Test (p. 72)

1	d		**9**	e
2	c		**10**	d
3	d		**11**	c
4	b		**12**	b
5	c		**13**	e
6	d		**14**	c
7	c		**15**	e
8	e			

⑨ Code and decode shapes

Practice box (p. 77)

1	e		**3**	d
2	d		**4**	a

⑩ Apply shape logic

Practice box (p. 79)

1	d		**3**	c
2	e		**4**	c

Standard 11+ non-verbal reasoning pull-out test

Section 1

1	a		**6**	c
2	c		**7**	e
3	c		**8**	b
4	e		**9**	d
5	d		**10**	e

Section 2

1	c		**4**	c
2	d		**5**	b
3	a		**6**	c

Section 3

1	b		**5**	c
2	c		**6**	d
3	e		**7**	e
4	e		**8**	b

Section 4

1	c		**5**	b
2	e		**6**	b
3	e		**7**	d
4	d		**8**	a

Section 5

1	c	6	b
2	e	7	a
3	c	8	b
4	d	9	b
5	e	10	d

Section 6

1	d	5	e
2	b	6	a
3	e	7	c
4	d	8	e

Section 7

1	b	6	a
2	d	7	e
3	e	8	c
4	d	9	b
5	d	10	c